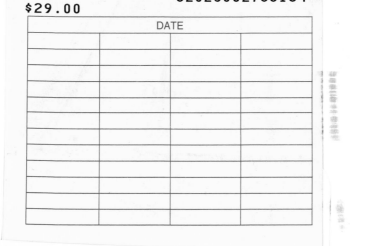

DATE			

BREAKING THROUGH

BREAKING THROUGH

STORIES and BEST PRACTICES FROM COMPANIES THAT HELP WOMEN SUCCEED

MARTINE LIAUTAUD

WITH FOREWORD BY CHRISTINE LAGARDE

WILEY

Library of Congress Cataloging-in-Publication Data:

Names: Liautaud, Martine, 1950– author.
Title: Breaking through / Martine Liautaud.
Description: Hoboken : Wiley, 2016. | Includes index.
Identifiers: LCCN 2016004195 | ISBN 978-1-119-26133-9 (hardback) |
   ISBN 978-1-119-26134-6 (Adobe PDF) | ISBN 978-1-119-26136-0 (epub)
Subjects: LCSH : Businesswomen. | Leadership. | Sex discrimination against women. |
   BISAC : BUSINESS & ECONOMICS / Leadership.
Classification: LCC HD6053 .L485 2016 | DDC 658.3/124082 – dc23
LC record available at   http://lccn.loc.gov/2016004195

COVER DESIGN: PAUL McCARTHY
COVER IMAGE: © DAVID MALAN (GETTY IMAGES)

Printed in the United States of America

10 9 8 7 6 5 4 3 2 1

CONTENTS

Contents

PART V
Ways to Help Entrepreneurs to Succeed

CHAPTER 20
Mentoring and Sponsoring Programs
163

CHAPTER 21
Networking
191

FOREWORD

> Women are increasingly seen, by men as well as women, as active agents of change: the dynamic promoters of social transformations that can alter the lives of both women and men.
>
> *Amartya Sen, 1999*

Despite Amartya Sen's astute pronouncement, women still lack opportunities to succeed—and become "dynamic promoters of social transformations." This is especially so for women in less developed countries who suffer daily injustices. But even in places where women fare relatively well, subtle—but inhibitive—forces hold us back: "traditional" gender roles; the specter of discrimination; and an ever-present glass ceiling.

As a result, women face a double disadvantage at work. Women are less likely than men to have a paid job: the difference between employed men and women—the gender gap—ranges from 12 percent in OECD (Organisation for Economic Co-operation and Development) countries to 50 percent in the Middle East and North Africa. To compound this, women who have jobs earn just three-quarters as much as men—even with the same level of education, and in the same occupation.

So, empowering women is certainly about fairness, but it is also about economic growth: 865 million women could contribute more to the global economy. If women were employed at the same rate as men, GDP would increase by 5 percent in the United States, by 9 percent in Japan, and by 27 percent in India. Closing these gaps would be transformative—and it can be achieved through what I have called the Three Ls:

- Learning: Investing in schools and making sure girls have a good education, especially in poorer countries.
- Labor: Supporting working women through parental leave, affordable and high-quality childcare, and taxes that do not discourage mothers from having a job.
- Leadership: Letting women show their true potential by rising to the top, based on their abilities and talents.

This third "L"—which rests not on policies but on women themselves—makes me especially honored to present this encyclopedia of insights into driving women's success. I know from personal experience that mentoring can help women find inspiration in one another, and draw confidence not only to break through the glass ceiling but also to make the most of the opportunity once they have it.

I want to see more women challenging themselves and testing their mettle. When they do, companies prosper: Fortune 500 firms with the best track records in raising women to prominent positions are significantly more profitable than average.

Perceptive and powerful, this book is essential reading for any woman who seeks to fulfill her true potential—and become, as Amartya Sen envisaged, an active agent of change.

Christine Lagarde
Managing Director
International Monetary Fund

ACKNOWLEDGMENTS

I AM GRATEFUL TO MY EDITOR RICHARD NARRAMORE for daring to think that a French businesswoman like me has something to say to America.

I would also like to thank the Women Business Mentoring Initiative team for their precious help, particularly my daughter Virginie Liautaud for her pivotal role in the interviews and Jean-Louis Duquesnoy, a true point man for this project as well as a long-time partner in my business and associative life.

My gratitude also goes to my sponsors and their representatives: Elisabeth Richard of ENGIE, Sofia Merlo of BNP Paribas, Eve Magnant of Publicis. They believed in this book from the beginning and gave me their friendly support throughout the process of writing and editing.

I must thank my husband Claude Liautaud for his backing on this project as for everything else. He knows how essential his love and support are in my life and my son Didier Liautaud whose contacts with the Stanford community were invaluable.

I extend special thanks to Elizabeth Carlassare, Pierre Khawand, and Dan Rudolf for their commitment and precious advice in finding the best way to publish this book.

And finally, I am deeply indebted to my good friend Dominique de La Garanderie, who is a staunch advocate for the empowerment of women.

PREFACE

MY FATHER WAS A BRILLIANT MAN who saw no difference in the intellectual potential of his children—boys or girls. Despite this, however, he was reluctant to see me choose a career, and my choice to become an entrepreneur would have been unimaginable to him.

But the values ingrained by my upbringing—for example, that we were expected to make an effort, overcome obstacles, and work toward our goals—helped me pursue my ambitions both as an employee in a large corporation, and later when I found my true role as an entrepreneur.

From the beginning of my career as an investment banker, I encountered skepticism from my predominantly male colleagues and business leaders. I was indeed one of the first women investment bankers in France.

People in the investment banking environment simply did not believe that I could succeed, and when I did, the bank's general director told me, "We thought that you would give up after six months at most." That same person thought he was giving me a compliment when he told me that despite my appearance, I had all the qualities of a man.

When I started working at that bank, my managers did not really help me: in fact, they specifically discouraged me from taking on existing clients. This turned out, however, to be a real opportunity, since the path was left open for me to pitch and approach all the other companies that were not yet clients, while leveraging the sizeable reputation and capabilities of the bank.

I started offering deals to foreign companies like the Japanese corporation Sony. These companies, on seeing a very young woman investment banker representing such a renowned banking institution (something which was extremely rare for them culturally), concluded that I had to be remarkable.

At the same time, I began to notice that top leaders at my client companies liked and trusted me. I was able to communicate with them in a clear and direct way that would have been less culturally acceptable coming from male colleagues.

It was apparent to me that businesses were not by nature hostile to women; they were simply not accustomed to seeing women take on large roles and responsibilities. I also began to see that courage and believing in your own capabilities are essential elements to succeed. In addition, finding yourself in uncharted territories can present big opportunities to stand out from the crowd while benefiting from external elements like your company's reputation.

Moreover, I also found out that being ready to face any ambitious challenge is key: I co-managed my investment bank's privatization team in the 1990s with this mindset. This team was in charge of very important matters like the privatization of France's TF1 television channel, which was the biggest channel at the time and is now the largest television network in Europe. The complexity of privatizing a public entity was new to all of us and encompassed both political and financial risks. As a result, candidates for positions related to privatization were not easy to find. I decided to dive into this new arena.

The experience I gained through this opportunity was essential to my career success. It is precisely these highly complex and challenging opportunities that can bring you the most satisfaction, rewards, and recognition when the outcome is successful. These opportunities also increase your confidence and experience. You learn the fundamental reality that it is easier to discuss new ideas with political, business, or other leaders than with their troops. True leaders are always interested in new ideas.

After my career successes with privatization and further developing my leadership abilities at Stanford University, I wanted to venture out on my own. My vocation as an entrepreneur was born.

I decided to acquire my first industrial company, Meccano, the leader in metallic construction toys. I also decided to create my own independent investment bank, Liautaud & Cie. During this period, I had the opportunity to negotiate the acquisition of Meccano by Mattel. Mattel wanted to make Meccano's construction toys the counterpart to the Barbie doll. I also helped Hervé de la Martinière create the publishing company Les Éditions de La Martinière, which has since become the second-largest publisher in France. I sold my shares in this publishing company to the Wertheimer family, owners of the Chanel fashion house.

When I started my own investment bank, it was not easy to build a competent team and find clients, like IBM or ENGIE, who would trust us. Indeed, many people in my field of investment banking did not understand my career or my choices, especially since I am a woman. After all, who would want to create their own company when they already had a successful career with a big bank? In fact, the president of the bank I was working for at the time told me that my decision was "pathetic," but that I could come back when I wanted to.

But once again, my efforts were rewarded, and large companies trusted us. In this book, you will see that large companies support and encourage women leaders, especially when their presidents and CEOs are convinced that women are essential to any business's success.

Looking back at my successful career at the time, I was satisfied to have been one of the pioneers and to have opened doors for other women. I always had a preference for teams that consist of both women and men with no distinctions made or special help needed.

But in 2009, I understood my mistake. At that time, there was a strong movement in France in favor of quotas for women on boards of directors, but I was not convinced at first that quotas were necessary. Indeed, I had been named as a board director at a young age and am still a board member for Savencia, one of the European leaders in dairy products, and for CentraleSupélec, a graduate education and research institute that is the result of the merger of two of France's leading engineering universities. However, I could only bow to the facts: women represented only 8 percent of board directors, and the numbers were not improving. The numbers were even worse for the proportion of women in top management at large companies! Let's not kid ourselves; the place of women in the business world is still an emerging market. I could not stand by doing nothing.

It was at this time that I, along with other Stanford University alumni, created the Women Business Mentoring Initiative, a nonprofit that supports women entrepreneurs in scaling up their companies. In December 2015, we launched the Women Initiative Foundation to support women in economic life even further, whatever their role.

My true conviction is that the world is full of opportunities created by the new economy. The new economy changes the balance of powers and gives both women and men the same chances.

However, everyone's success must be supported through mentoring and sponsoring activities, and women have generally had less access to business networks. It is the responsibility of all business leaders—women and men alike—who understand the power of mentoring and networking, to support women in their careers and business endeavors.

I am a good example of a woman who has benefited from embracing opportunities, facing challenges, and getting support from strong professional networks. Examples and stories from business leaders are fundamental in understanding how best to progress as an entrepreneur or employee.

Indeed, by advising founding presidents of large global companies, like Bouygues or Capgemini, I quickly came to realize that what sets them apart is their vision and energy. Moreover and more fundamentally, they are not afraid of failing. They understand that in the end, they will either succeed or, at the very worst, they will need to reinvent their business.

Women do not lack courage in life, and through our many roles in society we have acquired an inherent sense of adaptation. As a result, the modern world is made for us: don't be afraid to create businesses and to fail in these businesses. You will bounce back because you have that talent in you if you trust yourself and if you are not alone. Many networks can help you.

If you are a woman, don't ever believe that you are succeeding by luck. No, you are reaching your goals thanks to boldness, hard work, motivation, perseverance, and team spirit. Also remember that no one succeeds alone and that your oddness is also your strength.

It's true that my successes throughout my career must also be attributed to those who have supported me, inspired me, and opened doors for me. I would never have been able to succeed without them—and I am eternally grateful. In a similar way, I am grateful to Stanford University: without its professors, students, and unique and inspirational campus, none of my success would have been possible.

My experience at Stanford inspired me to start my own company and to commit time and energy to support women entrepreneurs, helping them succeed in their lives and their businesses, and contribute to the economy.

"It takes a village to raise a child." This African proverb can be applied to mentoring and networking—people working together to support each other for the benefit of both the individual and the collective. In this spirit, the Women Business Mentoring Initiative has mentored around 100 CEOs to date and, thanks to our partners, particularly ENGIE and BNP Paribas, we have extended our influence through business clubs in Paris and other regions of France, television programs, books, and executive training.

The Women Business Mentoring Initiative continues to grow: the main driver is the success of our women entrepreneurs. I firmly believe that, more than ever before, developing the talents of women, both as employees in companies and as entrepreneurs, is good for the economy, good for the country, and good for the world.

The purpose of this book is to both show you how useful mentoring is and to guide you through how to best take advantage of it. In addition, the book provides encouragement and inspiration for women entrepreneurs and leaders.

In the first part of the book, I discuss the new economy and the great range of opportunities it brings. Alongside this, I also look at the gender inequalities that continue to exist in the business world, and the forms of support that women employees and entrepreneurs need most.

One support mechanism is mentoring—and the networks it provides. I believe in mentoring and networking because I've benefited from them myself, both as an employee and as an entrepreneur. I am not the only one, as we will see in the interviews with international experts and CEOs of major companies that follow.

The remaining parts of the book develop this idea still further, focusing on the stories of women who have benefited from mentoring and sponsoring and who have leveraged their networks both as employees and as entrepreneurs.

Martine Liautaud

Part I

OVERVIEW

THIS BOOK DEMONSTRATES WOMEN'S GROWING economic power: they are the majority of the world's consumers, they are the engines of entrepreneurial growth, they represent 40 to 50 percent of the world's workers—but they are not yet represented in equal numbers in the top jobs or in equal numbers among the most successful entrepreneurs. We have also seen that women have courage, they take risks, they are innovative and creative, and do a lot with a little—they are efficient and collaborative, and bring new approaches to business. And those companies where women have made it to the top have witnessed tangible growth in their bottom line.

The added value of having women in the top jobs is recognized by the five major international companies (ENGIE, BNY Mellon, Publicis Groupe, BNP Paribas, and Oracle) that this book covers. These companies have set up programs designed to help their women employees break through to the top positions. ENGIE, a French multinational electric utility company, designed a program to develop women's professional careers, train more women directors and senior managers, and retain their talents. The program has not only achieved these aims but been transformational in changing mind-sets. BNY Mellon, an American multinational banking and financial services corporation, set up Women's Initiative Networking (WIN), and they have seen both a tangible increase in the number of women vice presidents, managing directors and executive committee members, and increased connectivity and collaboration across the company. Publicis Groupe, a French multinational advertising and public relations company, designed a program to retain talented women and develop their careers, and the company has seen more highly motivated employees, an improvement in teamwork and internal relationships, more effective management systems, and improved relationships with clients. BNP Paribas, a French multinational bank and financial services company, implemented its program in order to increase the number of women in the group's senior management and to benefit from the full capabilities and ambitions of its women employees. Its outcomes are quantitative: more than 20 percent of women in senior management achieved within the first three years. And Oracle, an American global computer technology corporation, developed a program both as a talent management tool to enable top talents to accelerate their professional growth and mentors to develop the leadership skills but also to increase the number of women in management roles.

At the heart of all these programs are mentoring and sponsoring. Both aim to develop women's potential and empower them to use the increasing opportunities that the new economy brings. Mentoring is about advice and guidance, it's about pointing out opportunities, suggesting new ways to take advantage of such opportunities, new ways of viewing the business landscape, new perspectives on old problems. But sponsoring goes further. Sponsoring is about championing mentees—opening doors and leading them through, introducing them and promoting them, speaking up for them, being on the lookout for opportunities and proposing them for new responsibilities and promotions. In sponsoring, sponsors put their necks on the line, use their own personal and professional capital, and take reputational risks for their mentees. And the results of sponsoring are the top jobs and the most successful entrepreneurs.

But this book shows us that, although women are increasingly mentored, men have traditionally been sponsored through the professional and personal networks they form more easily than women—for whom family commitments mean they are less able to create informal networks, for whom unconscious biases and stereotyping mean they have less confidence to put themselves up for jobs, and when they do, they are less often chosen, for whom lack of role models means lack of ambition, for whom lack of access to sponsors means lack of access to the top jobs.

It's now time to sponsor women—to continue to mentor them, but to structure sponsorship programs and integrate them into companies so that women are championed and get a shot at the top jobs. This is real equal opportunity. And as we begin to get increasing numbers of women at the top, as both employees and entrepreneurs, and as the networks these women form, and the role models they become, trickle down into our social structures and mores, we'll begin to see a change among our younger women and girls, and they'll ask themselves, *Why not me in the top job?*

1

Women and the New Economy

THE NEW ECONOMY GIVES WOMEN UNPRECEDENTED and exciting opportunities, but they can only take these opportunities—and have an equal chance of success—if they get the proper support. Using interviews and case studies, this book shows that for women employees and entrepreneurs, the most effective way to provide this support is through mentoring and sponsoring—and the networks and role models they provide.

Mentoring and sponsoring go hand in hand—and they are compelling because they help women get ahead. Mentoring is advising—how to accelerate your career or achieve your entrepreneurial goals. It's normally a relationship between a senior or more experienced mentor with a junior and less experienced mentee, but there are examples of reverse mentoring, with a junior mentor and a more senior mentee. Sponsoring is mentoring taken to the next level—sponsors champion their mentees, put them forward for promotion and positions of responsibility, or, in the case of entrepreneurs, introduce them to influential people, act as their referee, open doors.... In sponsoring, sponsors take a risk on their own reputation and put their necks on the line. But in both mentoring and sponsoring, the relationship is based on respect, confidentiality, and agreement on how to achieve goals.

THE NEW ECONOMY: OPPORTUNITIES FOR WOMEN

Statistics and pervading stereotypes suggest that we still have a long way to go in establishing gender equality. This is true, but by delving deeper into employment trends we find some indications that the new economy is helping women gain a more equal footing.

The Gender Gap

Huge progress has been made in the United States and Western Europe in establishing equality in educational attainment. In 2013 in the United States, more women than men enrolled in college. For OECD countries, 74 percent of women successfully completed upper secondary programs versus 66 percent for men in 2008.[1]

> In major corporations in the United States, women represent 53 percent of new hires but this decreases at each transition up the management ranks: only 37 percent of those promoted to managerial level are women, 26 percent vice presidents and senior executives, and only 14 percent on executive committees.

But in the workplace it's a different story, with most women only making it to the junior management levels and few achieving senior responsibility. In major corporations in the United States, women represent 53 percent of new hires, but this decreases at each transition up the management ranks: only 37 percent of those promoted to managerial level are women, 26 percent vice presidents and senior executives, and only 14 percent on executive committees.[2]

---

[1]http://unstats.un.org/unsd/demographic/products/socind/default.htm.
[2]www.mckinsey.com/features/women_matter.

Across all Organisation for Economic Co-operation and Development (OECD) countries, self-employed women earn 35 percent less than their male counterparts.

Outside of the corporate world, inequality persists in other forms. In the United States and Western Europe, women are more likely to work part-time and in less well-paid occupations. In the UK, nearly 40 percent of employed women work part-time (less than 30 hours a week) compared to just over 10 percent of men. The median wage gap between men and women remains significant: France (14 percent); Germany (17 percent); UK (17 percent) and the United States (18 percent).[3]

And it's the same story among the self-employed: across all Organisation for Economic Co-operation and Development (OECD) countries, self-employed women earn 35 percent less than their male counterparts. In the United States this figure is 43 percent (2011).[4] Yet it seems that the type of the work women do, and the time they have to devote to their business, provide only a partial explanation: it is still the case that many women spend more time on household work, leaving them less time for paid work and restricting the type of work they feel willing to take on.

The Opportunities of the New Economy

The new economy, led by rapid innovation in information technology and the spread of the Internet, is a revolution—a revolution that has created new business models and shattered the traditional roles of women and men.

The organizational structures and working practices of the old industrial and manufacturing economies no longer fit. Organizations have redefined themselves—their products, their services, their customers, their markets, and their income streams. Labels for this new economy, if used at all, include digital, social, sharing, and circular.

---

[3]www.oecd.org/gender/data/employment.htm.
[4]www.oecd.org/gender/data/entrepreneurship.htm.

> The organizational structures and working practices of the old industrial and manufacturing economies no longer fit.

The economic impact of new economy is striking. In the United States, e-commerce sales amounted to $300 billion in 2014, and are expected to grow to more than $400 billion in the next few years.[5] In France, a new website is set up every 30 minutes, and the number of e-commerce retailers grew by 17 percent between 2011 and 2012,[6] and more than doubled in 2013.[7] A Boston Consultancy Group study estimates that across all G20 countries, the new economy is set to grow at 8 percent each year, far outpacing growth in traditional sectors.[8]

Against this backdrop of upheaval and innovation, women have everything to play for—and everything to gain—and mentoring and sponsoring can help them to take these opportunities.

———

WOMEN IN CORPORATES AND FINANCE

In previous decades we used the term "glass ceiling" to describe the lack of women at senior executive and board level. But while glass ceilings still exist in the face of stereotypes and male networks, the phrases "leaking pipeline" or "frozen middle" are perhaps also appropriate when we see women falling behind as they go up the ladder of seniority.

> In Norway, where a "pink quota" was introduced in 2008, women now make up 36 percent of boards.

---

[5]For 2018, Forrester Research estimates $414.0 billion sales, and eMarketer estimates $491.5.

[6]On the 117,500 active online retailers in France in 2012, see Observatoire du numerique, chiffres clés 2013.

[7]An additional 138,000 online retailers were set up in France in 2013; see www.zdnet.fr/actualites/chiffres-cles-l-e-commerce-en-france-39381111.htm.

[8]https://www.bcgperspectives.com/content/articles/media_entertainment_strategic_planning_4_2_trillion_opportunity_internet_economy_g20/.

There is a growing understanding of the difficulties women face, and governments and corporations have taken active steps to redress the imbalance—and have made some progress. In Norway, where a "pink quota" was introduced in 2008, women now make up 36 percent of boards. In France, a law was passed in 2011 imposing progressive quotas for equal representation of women and men on boards of directors and steering committees: as a result, in 2013 women received 48 percent of new directorships (compared to 39 percent in 2012).[9]

But in the United States and UK, such moves have not been government-led—and both countries lag behind other developed economies. In 2013, only 16.9 percent of board seats in the United States were held by women;[10] this low figure has remained unchanged for the previous nine years. The UK was a similar story until a burst of activity following the 2011 Davies report,[11] which had an impact. Latest research from Cranfield School of Management reports 23.5 percent of women on boards in the FTSE (Financial Times Stock Exchange) 100—with only 17 more women on boards needed to reach the 2015 target of 25 percent. The FTSE 250 has also made great progress, more than doubling the percentage of women on their boards since 2011, from 7.8 percent to 18 percent.[12] Though far from gender parity, this represents a significant success in a relatively short space of time.

> Just 6 of the top 150 banks have female CEOs.

In the finance sector, the shortage of women at senior level is keenly felt. As set out in the *Financial Times* in 2014, just 6 of the

---

[9]Gouvernance 2013 (October 9, 2013), a study by the Cabinet Russel Reynolds Associates.
[10]www.catalyst.org/knowledge/2013-catalyst-census-fortune-500-women-board-directors.
[11]https://www.gov.uk/government/uploads/system/uploads/attachment_data/file/31480/11-745-women-on-boards.pdf.
[12]www.som.cranfield.ac.uk/som/dinamic-content/research/ftse/FemaleFTSEReportMarch2015.pdf.

top 150 banks have female CEOs.[13] And there are few examples of improvement—the number of women on the executive committees of large financial institutions rose just 3 percent between 2003 and 2013.

Encouragingly, however, many financial institutions are taking steps to redress this balance. In an industry that needs as much innovative thinking and constructive leadership as possible, institutions have recognized the long-term commercial benefits of tapping into the full potential of women as employees and senior business leaders. For example, Barclays set (and met) a target of having 20 percent of women on its board.[14] At BNY Mellon, promoting women at all levels has been built into their Corporate Social Responsibility program, with measurable results: since 2009 there has been a 100 percent increase in the number of women at Executive Committee, Operating Committee, and Regional Operating Committee levels.[15] Some of these figures do mask the fact that women tend to head up soft-skills departments and men income-generating ones, but the willingness of financial institutions to engage in promoting women in all fields is a step forward.

———

WOMEN IN STEM (SCIENCE, TECHNOLOGY, ENGINEERING, AND MATHEMATICS)

In STEM it is the action being taken to encourage more girls and women, rather than the numbers themselves, that suggests progress to a more equal future.

> Women in the United States earn 41 percent of STEM PhDs, but make up only 28 percent of tenure-track faculty.

———

[13] www.ft.com/intl/cms/s/0/56f28696-7949-11e4-9567-00144feabdc0.html#axzz3LJhM7K3E.
[14] http://fortune.com/2014/07/08/barclays-women-invest/.
[15] https://www.bnymellon.com/us/en/who-we-are/social-responsibility/campaign.jsp.

Women are historically underrepresented in STEM. Statistics released by the White House show that women in the United States earn 41 percent of STEM PhDs, but make up only 28 percent of tenure-track faculty. Over the past three decades, there has been a steep decline in the number of female graduates with computer science degrees. According to the U.S. Department of Education, the number of computer science degrees awarded to women peaked at 37 percent between 1984 and 1985 compared to only 18 percent in the period between 2008 and 2011.[16] As a consequence, women hold only 20 percent of all U.S. computer software engineer and computer programmer positions. In France, a report on managing gender and age diversity in IT teams (November 2013)[17] concluded that, at less than 25 percent, women were significantly under-represented. This report revealed that only 11.6 percent of women engineers were graduates in the new information and communications technologies (NTIC) in 2010.

Across developed nations, business, academia, and government are working to help girls and women overcome the social and psychological prejudices preventing them from pursuing careers in STEM. The New York Academy of Sciences launched the Global STEM Alliance,[18] a private-public partnership with industry, academic and educational institutions, government, and the nonprofit sector, aiming to provide resources, support, and mentoring for the next generation of STEM leaders.[19] Through a virtual platform, the initiative pairs students as mentees with international STEM expert mentors.

Showing what corporates can do, CISCO, a founding partner in US2020,[20] has pledged 20 percent of its workforce to spend 20 hours a year on STEM mentoring by the year 2020, with a

---

[16]http://energy.gov/sites/prod/files/2013/12/f6/Change%20the%20Equation%20Vital%20Signs%20Report%20December%202013.pdf.
[17]Survey conducted over a year by CIGREF (network of major companies) and the AFMD (French Association for Managers of Diversity) within member companies.
[18]www.nyas.org/WhatWeDo/ScienceEd/GlobalSTEM.aspx.
[19]www.nyas.org/WhatWeDo/ScienceEd.aspx.
[20]https://us2020.org/.

particular emphasis on encouraging girls and women.[21] In the UK, *Code First: Girls*, sponsored by the City of London and the Royal Bank of Scotland, inspired Abigail Holsborough, a young digital entrepreneur (see interview in Chapter 20), to take up coding and ultimately to found her first start-up.

WOMEN ENTREPRENEURS

The stereotype of female entrepreneurs is that they run small businesses in niche, low-profit areas of the economy. As with all stereotypes, there is an element of truth behind it. According to the Census Bureau Survey of Business Owners (2007),[22] 77 percent of women-owned enterprises were founded with $5,000 or less in capital. Nearly half of all women-owned firms were in service sectors, such as health care and social assistance (16 percent); professional, scientific and technical services (14 percent); and "other services" (16 percent).

> Entrepreneurship, across all sectors, is a real growth area for women in the new economy.

But, as with all stereotypes, this puts a negative spin on what can be interpreted as a positive development. Entrepreneurship, across all sectors, is a real growth area for women in the new economy. By offering women the opportunities and flexibility they don't always find in major corporations, entrepreneurship provides a new arena in which to pursue their ambitions. According to the 2007 Census, the number of women-owned businesses grew by 20 percent between 2002 and 2007, compared to 5.5 percent for men-owned firms.

---

[21] "The power of mentorship is more important today than ever to help young girls and women not only remain passionate about science, technology, engineering and math but also to believe that they, too, will be the future leaders in these fields" (Source: Christie Blair, "Cisco Blogs—Celebrating Girls in Technology—The Power of Mentorship," April 24, 2014).
[22] The 2012 report from the National Women's Business Council described the business cycle for women-owned firms in 2007.

The economic contribution of women-owned businesses is significant. The Center for Women's Business Research[23] measured the economic impact of the estimated 8 million U.S. businesses currently owned by women entrepreneurs at just under $3 trillion annually, which translates into the creation and/or maintenance of more than 23 million jobs—16 percent of all U.S. jobs. These jobs not only sustain the individual worker, but also contribute to the economic security of their families, the economic vitality of their communities, and the prosperity of the nation.

It is not clear what proportion of the sharing economy these women-owned businesses represent—this is fertile ground for further research. What is clear is that women choose to start businesses because working in this context is liberating and allows them to make direct changes to people's daily lives.[24]

> The comparatively low start-up costs of digital businesses is another positive for female entrepreneurs.

The comparatively low start-up costs of digital businesses is another positive for female entrepreneurs, who are less willing to take on debt than their male counterparts. Innovation and set-up in the digital economy have so far been predominantly male, but this is changing. Apple, Facebook, Microsoft, Yahoo! and Twitter are no longer typical, and the chance of success for women digital entrepreneurs is increasing. At the end of 2013, the French commission for Digital Women for a Digital Economy, in partnership with the French engineering school EPITA (École Pour l'Informatique et les Techniques Avancées), launched "Excellencia," an award for tech women. One of the three prizes awarded in September 2014 was given to a woman digital entrepreneur.

---

[23]Total economic impact of women-owned businesses in the United States: $2.8 trillion annually. Source: Center for Women's Business Research (National Women's Business Council), "The Economic Impact of Women-Owned Businesses in the United States."

[24]www.lelabo-ess.org/?Des-femmes-entreprennent-en-ESS, posted April 8, 2014.

Women Entrepreneur Networks

Many women entrepreneurs say that they feel isolated and lack networks. In the new economy, this is limiting. At a time when pace and visibility are key to success, networking is essential for sharing business information, gaining wider recognition, and marketing. Indeed, being undernetworked can significantly slow down the growth of new businesses.

> Networking is essential for sharing business information, gaining wider recognition, and marketing.

So given the proven importance of networking, why do women continue to lag behind?

Brigitte Gresy, French General Secretary of the Equality Council, believes that negative stereotyping and socialization are at the root. She suggests "Our society teaches boys to dare and girls to conform."[25] Diana Vanbrabant, Managing Director of ETACC (the European Training and Coaching Company),[26] offers another perspective. She says that men and women have different attitudes towards networking: women are often better one-on-one listeners and invest more time in nurturing close relationships, while men engineer their networks for their own gain.

> Our society teaches boys to dare and girls to conform.

Shifting this attitude is essential for women's success. It can only be done if we start to tackle the stereotypes and find more innovative ways to help women overcome professional obstacles. Numerous measures are already underway, such as positive discrimination, quotas, industry-led school programs and mentoring-sponsoring networks.

---

[25] Groupe Eyrolles, "Culture Mentoring," (2015), 51.
[26] Diana Vanbrabant, "How Do Women Network Differently from Men?" *The Next Women—Business Magazine*, September 20, 2012.

2

Mentoring and Sponsoring: The Keys to Success

MENTORING AND SPONSORING ARE COMPELLING in the context of the new economy because they are consistently effective in helping women get ahead. This is true regardless of participants' specific objectives, industries, or roles. To understand why this is the case, let's first look at what mentoring and sponsoring actually are.

Mentoring covers a vast range of programs and schemes. At its core, mentoring is a relationship between the mentor and the mentee. It's based on mutual respect, total confidentiality, and a shared understanding of how to achieve the mentee's objectives. Mentors use their own professional experience to advise mentees on how to accelerate their careers or achieve their entrepreneurial goals. Sponsoring is a step beyond mentoring—it's mentoring taken to the next level: the sponsor champions the mentee, suggests and supports their promotions, puts them forward for positions of responsibility and, especially for entrepreneurs, opens doors, acts as a reference, uses their networks to create opportunities, and then supports them to take these opportunities. In sponsoring, sponsors risk their own reputations and effectively put their necks on the line.

> Sponsoring is a step beyond mentoring—it's mentoring taken to the next level. . . . In sponsoring, sponsors . . . effectively put their own necks on the line.

The benefits of mentoring and sponsoring are tangible. Take the example of small businesses in the United States. Research shows that small businesses receiving three or more hours of mentoring achieve higher revenues and increased business growth compared to those that don't. Seventy percent of small businesses receiving mentoring or sponsoring survive more than five years—double the survival rate of nonmentored businesses.[1]

The difference, though, is that men find their informal mentors or sponsors through their own networks, while women lack the time and confidence to do the same. That's why, for women, structured and formal mentoring/sponsoring programs provide greater support, especially in the new economy, where career paths are being forged for the first time.

MENTORING AND SPONSORING WOMEN EMPLOYEES

All mentoring and sponsoring is personalized. This works to women's advantage because it allows them to focus on tackling the specific problems they face in the workplace and gain crucial support. With fewer role models higher up the organization, a mentoring/sponsoring program becomes their opportunity to discuss career progress. And, as part of the process, mentors—often senior managers—throughout an organization become more aware of the challenges women face.

Mentoring or sponsoring programs can take different forms depending on the objectives. A common constellation in larger organizations is an older mentor with a younger and less experienced mentee, as seen at ENGIE since 2010. Here, the objective may be to resolve a specific problem, such as retaining talent or encouraging more women into senior positions—and there are

---

[1]Source: U.S. Small Business Administration website, https://www.sba
.gov/blogs/why-mentor-key-small-business-growth-and-survival-0/?January
MentorCampaign.

benefits on both sides. The mentee learns more about company policy and culture, and the mentor raises his or her own profile amongst other senior managers.[2]

Another mentoring/sponsoring structure is the reverse: having a much younger mentor and a more experienced mentee. The idea here is to provide senior managers with the digital or market knowledge of the millenials, or to give them a young or new recruit's perspective on the organization. Since 1999, General Electric has been running such a program; Orange, Danone, Accenture, BNY Mellon, and IBM have followed suit.[3]

Mentoring and sponsoring programs can help induct new recruits but are also useful to support women returning to work after a long period of absence—whether due to maternity leave or training. Such programs smooth the transition back to work, bringing both the organization and the individual up to speed and providing reassurance that the new setup will work.

There are other reasons to set up a mentoring/sponsoring program: cross-department, cross-company, or cross-sector mentoring/sponsoring can promote knowledge creation. In this case, the pairs are two individuals doing the same job in different departments, companies, or sectors. Such programs have been shown to be particularly effective for high potential women, or women who already hold posts of responsibility, helping them share experiences and good practice when dealing with situations still largely dominated by men.

Mentoring and Sponsoring in the U.S. Military

Emulating the business sector, the U.S. military has begun to institute formal mentoring programs for women and minorities. A report by Major Darrell Adams in 1999 describes mentoring

(continued)

---

[2]Ibid.
[3]http://business.lesechos.fr/directions-ressources-humaines/management/developpement-personnel/avez-vous-un-reverse-mentor-57797.php.

(*continued*)

as an effective strategy to strengthen organizational success and enhance careers, including higher pay, promotions, opportunities to occupy leadership positions, and job satisfaction. Research in the report shows a high consensus (98 percent) that a mentoring relationship helped the respondent perform his or her job better and its importance to promotion success (86 percent). Mentors were credited with enhancing the protégés' competency and self-worth through counseling and pep talks (93 percent) and protecting them from organizational pressures (48 percent). While this study was small, the positive effects listed by women warrants further research as women assume greater responsibilities within the military.

Source: "Mentoring Women and Minority Officers in the U.S. Military," a research paper presented to the Research Department Air Command and Staff College in partial fulfillment of the graduation requirements of ACSC by Major Darrell E. Adams, March 1997.

MENTORING AND SPONSORING WOMEN ENTREPRENEURS

Mentoring/sponsoring programs focused exclusively on women entrepreneurs are not yet well developed. Programs such as the Paris Initiative Enterprise work with men and women entrepreneurs, the Paris-based Women Entrepreneurs Network and Berlin-based WEFOUND offer events and workshops for women, but not specific mentoring programs. Other examples include mentoring circles set up by nonprofits such as WBMI (Women Business Mentoring Initiative), European PWN (Professional Women's Network), and Federation Pioneers. These nonprofit organizations lead the way in mentoring and sponsoring women, but there is much scope for expansion.

The case for mentoring and sponsoring is clear. Done effectively, they transform careers, and help employees and entrepreneurs contribute more to their organizations and the economy.

In the digital age, electronic mentoring—facilitated by e-mail exchanges, discussion forums, and online chat rooms—could be one solution. This can be helpful especially if the mentor and mentee are geographically far apart, but nothing beats meeting face to face to establish the trust so essential to a successful mentoring and sponsoring relationship.

The Future

The case for mentoring and sponsoring is clear. Done effectively, they transform careers, and help employees and entrepreneurs contribute more to their organizations and the economy. They particularly help women because they provide women with the professional networks they are not always in a position to forge themselves.

In the context of the new economy, the case for women-focused mentoring and sponsoring programs becomes even stronger. The precedent as to how women can best seize the diverse opportunities created by the new economy is constantly being set and reset. As the interviews with professional women in the following chapters confirm, it is the personalized focus inherent to mentoring and sponsoring that goes furthest in supporting women as they navigate this previously unknown terrain.

Part II

VOICES OF WOMEN BUSINESS LEADERS

THE RANGE OF VIEWS PRESENTED in this part can be summarized in a few clear and constructive messages:

- Entrepreneurialism is not gender specific: women, as well as men, have the talent to create and develop companies.
- Women are a rich resource for companies—and companies that have understood this are now more productive and equitable.
- Women are the victims of negative stereotyping: this comes from cultural inequalities and is increasingly apparent to both women and men; but measures to redress this may be seen as tough (such as quotas) and are not always implemented.
- Mentoring, in all its forms, can leverage this situation: for both women entrepreneurs and women employees, it's the most effective way for women to break through the glass ceiling and mend the leaky pipeline.

3

Obstacles to Success and Solutions for Overcoming Them

IT'S CLEAR THAT WOMEN ARE NOT EQUALLY represented in companies or among entrepreneurs—they are in the minority everywhere, or at least they're a minority in key decision-making posts, rare in the senior levels of management, and almost completely absent in executive committees and at the board level of major groups. Yet they represent at least 50 percent of the work force—and even if many women set up and lead SMEs (Small and Medium Enterprises), they're not in the high-growth sectors or present among the leading entrepreneurial companies. The distribution is so uneven that even the most sexist members of society admit that it can't only be attributed to lack of talent or work ethic.

In Part II, we highlight the main social and cultural obstacles that prevent women from getting to the top, and provide solutions as to how to get around them.

We asked six experts to help us analyze the persistence of gender inequality in business—and how we can find a way around these obstacles.

Our experts are highly acclaimed in their respective fields, and, through their actions and thinking, they exert a strong influence on public opinion. They are all deeply committed to ensuring that women achieve their rightful place in business life.

Whether they are professors in universities, chief executives, headhunters, or event organizers, not one of them has ever lost sight of the obstacles they had to overcome to reach the positions they now occupy.

What they tell us is a mine of information and in-depth analysis on the gender gap in business. But more than that, our experts lead us to conclude that a clear corporate policy to reverse gender inequality can quickly and significantly change mind-sets and reality.

THE OBSTACLES

The first obstacle is in the heads of women themselves.

Women in the workforce today were raised in the inherited roles of gender difference. Through their upbringing and in their schools, they absorbed an intellectual and cultural set of values in which power and money is the responsibility of men, and raising children is the responsibility of women. Men, who are still the decision makers in business life, were raised with the same values and hold to the idea that women have to make a choice between family or work—and taking on both is contradictory. This upbringing leads to a series of prejudices, which Audra Bohannon (senior partner at Korn Ferry) lists for us: women are not assertive enough to assume leadership roles, they're too emotional, they're more tactical than strategic, and so on.

These prejudices are dangerous because, as Valérie Bernis (executive VP at ENGIE) tells us, it means women spontaneously choose the roles of specialist or expert—advisory roles—and not the more visible roles of general manager or leader.

If any progress has been made—and it has—it's because both men and women are beginning to see these prejudices as stereotypes.

And this is a good first step—because behind the stereotype is bias.

Research tells us the decision-making behavior is influenced by biased reasoning, based on false hypotheses, prejudices, or assumptions. For example, the assumption that a mother will refuse a job where the hours don't fit with family life means that she isn't even offered the job. Interrupting a woman when she is speaking in a meeting—and Margaret Neale (professor at Stanford University) thinks this happens a lot—is more acceptable than interrupting a man. And women's upbringing has not prepared them to object to such rudeness. Although a man will use every means to make himself heard, a woman will usually keep quiet, and her ideas or proposals will not be heard—and what an opportunity the meeting will miss. Margaret Neale also tells us that men and women are treated differently in appraisals, and that any benefit of the doubt will be given to men but almost never to women, mainly because criteria used in appraisals are biased towards men, and lead to the unexpected consequences of good intentions.

Deborah Gillis (president and CEO of Catalyst) tells us that women don't have any access to the "hot jobs"—visible jobs that carry power, such as international roles, senior positions in the finance or budget departments, responsibility for major teams. This means there are no role models—so the vicious circle of gender inequality keeps on turning. One of the reasons this happens is that women don't find influential sponsors—who, by advocating and taking a risk on someone, can make a career. Christiane Bergevin (Executive VP at Desjardins Group—Canada) gives us an amusing, but very typical, example of this impossible encounter (Chapter 8).

All these obstacles make up the famous glass ceiling. Though women are around 50 percent of the workforce in the United States, though they exceed men in terms of qualifications at university level, though they control 73 percent of American household spending, they manage only 5 percent of companies in the S&P 500 and hold only 19.2 percent of directorships in the same sample. Above all, women earn significantly less than men with identical backgrounds, education, and experience.[1]

Other obstacles, sometimes more trivial, stand in the way of women entrepreneurs.

In this world of rapid technological change and new business models, networks are, more than ever before, sources of information, exchange, and opportunities. For a range of reasons, women have fewer networks and benefit less from them than their male counterparts. Cultivating this form of social capital is encouraged in men, while women feel guilty about spending any time on networking and therefore less time with their families.

Among other psychological obstacles preventing women's success is their tendency to want to know something, rather than be known for it. We would not go so far as to say it's the opposite for men, but it is true that men are more likely to draw attention to their achievements and their ambitions than women.

Access to finance is an obstacle rarely highlighted but it exists—and not only in developing countries. Inequality in terms of finance is present everywhere, and the United States is no different, as Irene Natividad (president of the Global Summit of Women), tells us. We see that banks are more likely to lend to men because men have a different attitude to debt than women. But the different treatment does not stop with banks—venture capital funds also extend a better welcome to projects headed by men than by women.

———

THE SOLUTIONS

Many of the solutions can be found in the obstacles themselves.

If prejudices are so strong, and have such consequences, can we get rid of them? And if so, how?

The answers are age old: but they are based on lack of awareness and lack of will.

Today's women are far more informed than their mothers about gender inequality—not only in social life, but also in economic life.

---

[1]Deborah Gillis (Chapter 6). Women earn $4,600 less than men from their very first post-MBA job, a gap that widens with time.

In addition, there are more women in the job market, and work isn't simply a supplementary salary but a means of personal and professional development—and the means to financial autonomy. More informed, and more ambitious, women are therefore sensitive to the gap between them and men. At the same time, their investment in a working life has made their demands more visible, and what used to be a feminist issue, is now a social issue.

The obstacles can be overcome by a two-pronged approach: collective and individual.

The first is political—in the wider sense. This includes structural decisions that create a sustainable change on the landscape in favor of women.

The fight against stereotypes has become a national issue in a number of developed countries: educational programs, television broadcasts, laws and regulations checked with a fine toothcomb to ensure that all traces of discrimination are eliminated.

In addition to these general measures are more targeted efforts to encourage a greater number of young girls to choose STEM (science, technology, engineering, and math) subjects, an area that currently has a majority of men but that opens up career prospects in innovative and exciting areas for women.

Christine Lagarde (managing director of the International and Monetary Fund) reminds us that education in developing countries is a means of emancipation and equality for young girls.

In terms of salary, the California Fair Pay Act, which took effect as of January 1, 2016, and which could be imitated in other states, aims to make it easier for employees to contest wage inequalities, and guarantees equal pay for equal work.

The policy on quotas is another example of political will. Several European countries have passed and enforce laws for more equal representation of women in boards of directors. Wherever these measures have been taken, there have been spectacular results. As Irene Natividad puts it in the 2015 Corporate Women Directors International report, "quotas *are working* to accelerate women's access to board seats."[2] In France for example, where the

---

[2] 2015 "CWDI Report: Women Board Directors of Fortune Global 200: 2004–2014," pp. 4, 9. http://globewomen.org/CWDInet/?page_id=15.

situation had been similar to that in the United States, the number of directors increased significantly, and the aim of 40 percent of women directors on board by 2017 will very probably be achieved.

To make sure that this movement is not only limited to women at the top of the pyramid, we also need to see strategies voluntarily implemented throughout companies and the inclusion of gender diversity into corporate governance codes.[3] Most of the world's major groups have set up equality and diversity programs to eliminate inequalities in their workforces. Programs aimed at closing the gender gap demonstrate a diverse range of actions. Thus, for example, we see major groups—and not so major groups—financing crèches or reviewing their appointment and promotion criteria so as not to penalize women returning to work after maternity leave. Similarly, companies modify their criteria for selecting employees with high potential by not restricting their choice to the 28-to-32 age group, where women are under-represented because of child rearing.

On a more individual note, women are becoming more involved in networking and mentoring in all their forms—from classical mentoring to reverse mentoring and to intercompany mentoring. Several examples of these programs and their outcomes are presented in Part III.

In the same spirit, companies are developing sponsoring programs, particularly focusing on high-potential women. Irene Natividad, in another area, tells us about her "political mothers"—those sponsors who taught her everything and who invested in her to make her become the woman of influence that she is today.

For this movement to produce convincing results, it has to be shared at all levels of the corporation, and men have to be actively involved.

Valérie Bernis, executive vice president at ENGIE, summarizes the benefits of mentoring as a tool for developing the company through the development of its workers:

> One of those tools—mentoring—stands out, with at least three virtues: helping mentees achieve their goals, including,

---

[3]Ibid., 10.

but not only, top management posts; establishing mentors firmly in their responsibility; and proving that not only human beings, but also human relationships, have their place at the heart of the company—and even that those relationships are a criterion of performance.

Many of the speakers in this book demonstrate to what extent this vision meets reality, and the effectiveness of gender equality actions when they are implemented with intelligence and generosity.

4

Role of Women in the Global Economy

INTERVIEW WITH IRENE NATIVIDAD, FOUNDER AND PRESIDENT OF GLOBAL SUMMIT OF WOMEN

The goal is to unleash women's economic power whether it's entrepreneurial or corporate.

What role do women play in the global economy?

What I have seen is that women's economic power has grown. It's not at the top yet—women are not yet CEOs or senior executives in large numbers, but women form the base of every economy in the world including the United States, because they are now 40 to 50 percent of the world's workers. Because women are making money, they are now the majority of consumers with tremendous buying power, and women are the engine behind entrepreneurial growth in every country of the world.

In the United States, 40.4 percent of small businesses are owned by women. These businesses generate 2.3 trillion USD worth of revenues yearly and hire 8 million people in the United

States. If you take away women workers, if you take away women consumers, if you take away the buying power and production power of women-owned enterprises, economies of the world would collapse.

> Women are the engine behind entrepreneurial growth in every country of the world.

Overall, I think entrepreneurship is the avenue for women to gain a level playing field because they can become their own bosses. Right now, 80 percent of microentrepreneurs globally are women and some will grow to become SMEs.

Therefore, given the fact that women are the growth sector in every corner of the economy, they will drive the twenty-first century economy. In fact, Booz & Co. did a study they called the "Third Billion," which showed that if you unleash women's economic power, primarily in emerging economies, it is equal to India's and China's economies combined. Thus, the goal is to grow that power, whether it's entrepreneurial or corporate, not just to benefit the women, but to foster the economic growth of their countries.

> If you unleash women's economic power, primarily in emerging economies, it is equal to India's and China's economies combined.

What assets would you say women managers or entrepreneurs have?

Women have courage; they take risks. Women went to school when everybody said, "You can't." Women created businesses without access to credit. They created enterprises that nobody ever thought of. They entered corporate leadership without role models. Incrementally, they made themselves an economic power without their realizing.

I think women are innovative; they are creative; and I am very proud of them precisely because they do a lot with so little, and often without the love and support of the very people who say they care for them.

What would you say are the most common stereotypes about women and women in business?

I don't really like to talk about stereotypes because all it does is perpetuate them. However, one major misperception is that women are incapable of leadership since they cannot focus due to family responsibilities. There is a sense among some corporate leaders that women's concern for the family makes them seem not serious, not ambitious enough, not driven enough to be successful. But that stereotype is totally false. There are lots of very driven, talented, ambitious women who are stopped by structure, by prejudices, by misperceptions that they did not create. So it's not a question of talent supply. It's a question of demand on the part of companies and institutions to make women's talent really become realized and grow to the fullest.

How can we improve the place of women in the economy? What do you think about quotas?

On the corporate leadership side, I am a strong believer in quotas because what they do is accelerate the process. As Michel Landel of Sodexo said, "They are a jolt to the system"—they force companies to look and ask, "Where are the women?" Quotas are not made to be in place forever, but they are a door that women must push open and take advantage of. It is a door that allows companies to look for the women within their own ranks and see where they are. All business functions by way of targets—sales targets, recruitment goals, and so forth, so why not set targets for gender diversity within a company? That's what quotas do—create a target by law so companies will abide by them.

> On the corporate leadership side, I am a strong believer in quotas because what they do is accelerate the process.

In terms of women entrepreneurs, we need to provide them with financing to start and to grow their enterprises. Access to credit is the biggest impediment to women entrepreneurs, no matter what country you happened to be in, including the United States. Until the Center for Women's Business Research released their study aggregating women-owned companies' impact on the U.S. economy, banks and the government didn't pay attention. This NGO and other women's business groups also pressed on the government to provide sex-disaggregated data on SMEs, as well as to provide support in terms of training and loans to enable women-owned businesses to be sustainable.

What do you think about mentoring programs? Do you think they're efficient?

I think mentoring is necessary, but mentoring programs are a first step. I want mentoring to grow to sponsorship. Women are mentored, but men are sponsored. Sponsorship means that a senior person uses his/her capital to advance somebody that he/she believes in. Mentoring is important but not good enough. In small businesses, though, mentoring is key, especially when an enterprise is transitioning from a start up to a viable business.

> Sponsorship means that a senior person uses his/her capital to advance somebody that he/she believes in.

With regard to mentoring programs in large companies, I would like to point out that not all mentoring relationships go well and mentoring programs have to be closely supervised. One of the things that I have found to work is something called cross-industry mentoring. This type of mentoring works because there is privacy. Not every woman feels comfortable saying everything to a mentor within the same company. For instance, in Spain, a group of Spanish businesswomen (from Oracle, American Express, and other companies) created their own model for cross-industry mentoring. They set up the infrastructure in order to prevent sexual harassment, to establish real outcomes, and to make sure it was productive overall.

Because this program gave women privacy, the businesswomen who created the program felt that it was even better than the more classic internal mentoring programs. It also opened participating women's eyes to other companies and other possibilities. The founders worked very hard to make sure that the relationships between mentors and mentees were good and also that companies didn't rob talent from another company. The group took a year to make this program happen, but I think that what they created was probably a better mentoring model. Women are always fearful that what they say to their mentor can get out, and they often hold back.

Did you have a mentor or mentors in your career? Were you a mentor, or are you a mentor?

Before being head of the Summit, I was president of the National Women's Political Caucus. You had to be elected for that position, and it was a big process. During my two terms, I had three political mothers whom I admired. One was Asian-American, Patsy Mink, and she was the author of the legislation that opened doors for women in sports and education. Every American woman athlete points out that Title IX (which Patsy co-sponsored and fought for) enabled her to be here but they don't know who was behind this law. It was Patsy Mink from Hawaii, the first nonwhite member of Congress. The other one was Shirley Chisholm, the first African-American woman member of Congress, who was from New York, where I'm from. She was a civil rights leader, with a powerful voice literally and figuratively, who ran for president. The third was a white woman, Bella Abzug, who worked hard to have women NGOs (nongovernmental organizations) have a voice within the United Nations, and who fought for women's rights while in Congress.

These women were strong, and they had influence and national impact beyond the districts to which they were elected. Everybody knew who they were. I felt privileged that they would invest in me. They have since passed on, but I learned a great deal from them. All of them were eloquent speakers who could move audiences to follow them. All had a presence that couldn't be ignored. All of them took risks that cost them from time to time, but they persevered. They were not just passive members of Congress. They pushed for changes that were national in scope. I think I get my energy from them and the will to keep going.

If I can help somebody, I just do it within my little universe.

I'd like to think I'm a mentor to women in the context of the Summit, hundreds of whom I am privileged to meet each year at the Summit. Every year I try to tell them what to do with their careers. Go try that, go meet that person, go over there and be noticed. If somebody asks me if there is somebody that you can recommend for a board seat, I am always ready to help and bring up some woman's name. Then, I give my advice to the person I recommended. I just do it automatically now—I don't even think about it. It's not a formal relationship but if I can help somebody, I just do it within my little universe.

5

Career Strategies for Women

INTERVIEW WITH PROFESSOR MARGARET NEALE, ADAMS DISTINGUISHED PROFESSOR OF MANAGEMENT AT STANFORD GRADUATE SCHOOL OF BUSINESS

> Adding women to teams makes the teams more effective at collective action.

In your view, what female stereotypes still prevail in our society? What are the perceptions of women in business?

Well, I think the stereotypes have changed very much. We all stereotype—and both men and women stereotype women. I want to be really clear that the evidence—empirical evidence in research—suggests that it's not that men see us one way and women see women in different ways; we see each other the same way; we've been socialized in the same system of social norms and mores, and as a result the behaviors that are often identified as making it difficult for women to succeed flow from perceptions of both men and women about women.

> The behaviors that are often identified as making it difficult for women to succeed flow from perceptions of both men and women about women.

Do you think that there is still gender inequality in business organizations?

Yes, but I typically see the gender inequality based on a sense of organizations or individuals needing to keep women in their place. This overt sexism — "women don't belong here" — is actually relatively rare. Of course there are always a few very visible exceptions — there was a recent *Newsweek* article about what Silicon Valley thinks about women, focusing on the lack of women in venture capital firms — but let's put that aside for a minute (Burleigh 2015).

Gender inequality is more likely to flow from the imposition of nonconscious biases that are much more subtle, but their presence makes it systematically more difficult for women to get promoted. And we have lots of empirical evidence to support the contention that these systematic biases reduce the likelihood that women will advance in organizations — not because of their performance, but because of their gender.

> Gender inequality is more likely to flow from the imposition of nonconscious biases.

One of the most powerful examples of this was a study that was published in the *American Economic Review* by Goldin and Rouse in 2000. They looked at the hiring process of symphony orchestras. Why would the leaders of a symphony orchestra care whether it's a woman or a man playing the violin; what they care about is the quality of the music. So because the music, the performance, of the person is what's important, you might expect the impact of gender discrimination to be minimal. What these researchers found was quite the opposite. When aspiring musicians auditioned behind a screen, women were 50 percent more likely to move to the second round of auditions and were 1.6 times more likely to win an orchestral position compared to women who did not audition behind a screen.

The evaluators judged the female-generated music as less worthy when they knew it was a female. When they did not know the gender of the musician, it dramatically changed how women's performance was evaluated. Making the gender of the musician unknown changed the outcome.

Second, men and women are treated differently in evaluations. Consider the tenure process at universities. There are standards of performance. Using sports metaphors, we often question where the candidate "cleared the bar." If someone's record reveals that they are so far above the bar that the bar is really irrelevant, then male or female, it doesn't make any difference—we're going to tenure that person. If their record indicates that they cannot clear the bar, don't make it to the bar, then we're not going to tenure them—male or female. The issue is what happens when they are right at the bar. Now it is a judgment call. Here is where we run into trouble. If we hold the standards very tightly for women, we say, "Well, she didn't actually clear the bar so we're going to deny her promotion." But, because we have a lot more experience with men, some of whom received tenure and went on to outstanding performance, and some who were tenured and went on to mediocre performance, we are more likely to give him "the benefit of the doubt." When we do that, if you play that out systematically, what happens is you create the exact organization that we find ourselves with at the moment—where there's lots of women in the lower ranks, and there are very few at the top. It doesn't take much; all we have to do is to make a slight adjustment in leeway around how we apply the standard—and we get the effect. So the question is *Are we giving people an equal benefit of the doubt?*

What are the strategies that women can use in the workplace to increase their power, navigate their way through the organization, and ultimately thrive in the workplace?

We can look at strategies that are macro strategies and micro strategies. The macro strategy requires us to consider the criteria that organizations use to screen applicants: for example, do criteria discriminate poor performers from good performers, or do they discriminate on something other than performance? Consider what happened at Carnegie Mellon University (Fischer and Margolis 2002). Computer science majors were overwhelmingly male—and the university administration and faculty were trying to figure out why. One of the things they realized was a criterion for admittance to the program was that a student had to have extensive computer and coding experience. They asked themselves, *Is this experience really necessary for performance in the major? Can't we teach coding? Can't we provide internships for experience?*

> With a very disciplined eye, assess the criteria you are using to move people into the organization or up the organization.

When they revised the criteria for admissions to reflect the set of demands that the people must meet to get into the major, within a very short period of time, 40 percent of the majors were women. And they didn't suffer in terms of quality—they didn't say that they're lowering the bar—they were just saying, "Can we teach this?" And the answer was, "Yes, you can teach that, it doesn't need to be an entry criterion."

So with a very disciplined eye, assess the criteria you are using to move people into the organization or up the organization. Ask yourself, *Do we use that criteria because we've always used that criteria? Or are the criteria we use, in fact, the criteria that discriminate between successful and nonsuccessful performance?*

So that's one of the strategies that we can use as employers, or as organizations. How do you feel about things like positive discrimination or quotas? Do you think they have a place in promoting women?

The first thing I'd want to do is make sure that the criteria we use in our organizations are valid. That is, they reflect the skills, knowledge, and abilities that we need for successful performance. Then, you don't have to positively discriminate. You just take out the criteria that are discriminatory—if you think about this, women have been the majority of our college graduates (I don't know if this is global but it's true in the United States) for the last 20 years. And so the question is *Are you really lowering any criteria, or are you benefiting one group to the exclusion of the other?* If you have the criteria correctly identified, then you dramatically improve the likelihood that you will identify qualified talent, regardless of their race, gender, or age. It turns out that Stanford actually overadmits women from the MBA pool in comparison to the percentage of women in the MBA pool. You might call this an example of positive discrimination. And I have had people ask me, "Does that mean that Stanford is admitting women who are less qualified?" And the answer is no—for two reasons. First, we have over 5,000 applicants for 400 positions. We could reject the bottom 3,500 and then just randomly select 400 people from the remaining 1,500 and get a great class.

> There is a consistent finding that adding women to teams makes the teams more effective at collective action.

So if you have the luxury, as Stanford does, of having so many people applying, then you can pick the class in a way to make the class better off. And that is the second point. There is a consistent finding that adding women to teams makes the teams more effective at collective action—and it turns out there is a lot of research that says that when classes are in teams—it's at team level—when teams are functioning in socially diverse environments, their performance is better (Wooley, Chabris, Pentland, Hashmi, and Malone 2010). So having more women on teams seems to make the teams more effective. So let's design for innovation and effectiveness rather than for homogeneity.

The interesting thing is that if you look at organizations—most organizations are at, or close to, parity at the lower levels. But the demography looks quite a bit different at the executive levels. That is where the huge disparity exists. In many respects, you already have the pool (the lower level); so let's now talk about what an individual can do.

I would recommend your readers go to the *New York Times*, where there's been a series of interesting thought-out pieces by Adam Grant and Sheryl Sandberg. They talk about how to get your voice heard, and they have nicely written, research-based discussions about the challenges that women face. In particular, they suggest strategies that a number of us have been using to help women get their voices heard in their organizations and getting credit for the insights that they bring to the table. There's a big problem in that women are more likely to be interrupted when they speak, and that any ideas generated by a women aren't given equivalent consideration as those very same ideas voiced by a man.

One strategy that an increasing number of teams and organizations are adopting is the "no interruption" rule.

> The idea of the "no interruption" rule is that everybody gets to get their idea out before there's an interruption.

What happens, oftentimes, is that a woman will begin to speak—and she will be interrupted before she can complete her thought. Let this happen often enough and even the most extraverted among us will simply give up trying to be heard. And so the idea of the "no interruption" rule is that everybody gets to get their idea out before there's an interruption. Very simple and actually quite a bit more civil than the testy retort of "Let me finish my thought." Certainly, I could have held my ground and as you interrupted, begin speaking louder and maybe even observe stridently, "Hold on a second, I'm not done!" But women are socialized to be more polite, so this is difficult to do time and time again. But with the "no interruption" rule, we now have a standard of civility that applies to all team members. It is not about women; it is about the ideas.

A second strategy relies on my teammates. If I say, "I have this really great idea," or I volunteer an idea and it doesn't get traction, it may be very difficult for me to argue, "That was a really good idea, you need to listen again." If I do, I am likely to get a negative response from my teammates for being so pushy. But if you and I are in the meeting, and you say, "What a great idea Maggie had—and I don't think we really heard it. So, Maggie, could you restate it again so that we can get the full sense of it?" You now get credit—and so do I. You get credit as someone who is paying attention and getting folks engaged in the conversation—so you're in a kind of leadership facilitation role that you get credit for—and I get credit for my idea. So part of this is like having a posse: have people there who, when you have a good idea, can support you. And it's not only another woman—men can do that too, and in fact it's effective when a man says to the team, "Hey, look. Maggie just said that, and I think we need to look at what her perspective is on that." So you are the champion for other people, and they are the champions for you. And you both get credit for it. And the point is that you get the benefit of being supportive of others. If I extol your virtues, that is certainly an acceptable behavior for me to engage in—I'm being supportive of my colleagues, I am helping the team, it's perfect—much better than acts of self-aggrandizement! And so I think we need to have those kinds of ideas in mind and be quite generous with the allocation of credit to other folk when it's deserved. And don't forget, this is all deserved. It's not like if it's a stupid idea I'm going to support it—then we'd both be diminished. But what I can also say is, "Wow! That sounds like just what Maggie said! So now I think we're getting a consistency—we've got Steve and Maggie suggesting the same course of action."

> In the evolution of today's organizations, we rarely fight the battle of access. What we are fighting now is the unintended consequences of good intentions. To do so requires discipline, vigilance, and leveraging our support networks.

So these small changes can have a big impact. What is important to understand is that, in the evolution of today's organizations, we rarely fight the battle of access. What we are fighting now is the unintended consequences of good intentions. To do so requires discipline, vigilance, and leveraging our support networks.

REFERENCES

Burleigh, Nina. "What Silicon Valley Thinks of Women." *Newsweek*, January 28. www.newsweek.com/2015/02/06/what-silicon-valley-thinks-women-302821.html.

Fisher, Allan, and Jane Margolis. 2002. "Unlocking the Clubhouse: The Carnegie Mellon Experience." *ACM SIGCSE Bulletin* 34, no. 2: 79–83.

Goldin, Claudia, and Cecilia Rouse. 2000. "Orchestrating Impartiality: The Impact of 'Blind' Auditions on Female Musicians." *American Economic Review* 90, no. 4: 715–741.

Grant, Adam, and Sheryl Sandberg. 2015. "Madam CEO, Get Me a Coffee." *New York Times*, February 6. www.nytimes.com/2015/02/08/opinion/sunday/sheryl-sandberg-and-adam-grant-on-women-doing-office-housework.html.

Grant, Adam, and Sheryl Sandberg. 2015. "Speaking While Female." *New York Times*, January 12. www.nytimes.com/2015/01/11/opinion/sunday/speaking-while-female.html.

Grant, Adam, and Sheryl Sandberg. 2014. "When Talking about Bias Backfires." *New York Times*, December 6. www.nytimes.com/2014/12/07/opinion/sunday/adam-grant-and-sheryl-sandberg-on-discrimination-at-work.html.

Woolley, A. W., C. F. Chabris, A. Pentland, N. Hashmi, and T. W. Malone. 2010. "Evidence for a Collective Intelligence Factor in the Performance of Human Groups." *Science* 330, no. 6004: 686–688.

6

Inclusive Leadership

INTERVIEW WITH DEBORAH GILLIS, PRESIDENT AND CEO OF CATALYST

It's time to redefine leadership for today's working world and build workforces and leadership teams that look like the communities we serve.

What is the role of women in today's economic world?

Women hold enormous economic power. They make up almost half the labor force in the United States, outpace men in earning advanced degrees, and control 73 percent of all household spending. Yet there's been glacial progress in closing the pay gap and advancing women to more senior roles. Less than 5 percent of CEOs in S&P 500 companies are women, and according to our 2014 Catalyst Census: Women Board Directors, women hold only 19.2 percent of board seats in S&P 500 companies. And while it seems obvious that women and men should be paid equally across all industries and regions, women still earn less than their male peers despite identical backgrounds, education, and experience. Catalyst research shows that women earn $4,600 less than men from their very first post-MBA job, a gap that widens with time. I first started talking about the pay gap as a high school senior, and it's frustrating to see that the gap has narrowed only marginally since that time.

> Women still earn less than their male peers despite identical backgrounds, education, and experience.

But I'm confident that change is on the horizon. In my extensive travels around the world for Catalyst, I've seen a greater public awareness of and willingness to discuss equal opportunities at work than ever before—and a greater demand to forge a better workplace for everyone.

Do women managers bring any particular advantages to the company?

Study after study has shown that having more women on boards and in senior leadership, on average, improves financial performance, drives innovation, and enables organizations to better serve their customers. It's also linked to increased philanthropy and corporate social performance. So this is not simply a women's issue. What's good for women is good for business, families, communities, economies, and society at large.

> Study after study has shown that having more women on boards and in senior leadership, on average, improves financial performance, drives innovation, and enables organizations to better serve their customers.

To be successful, companies must make sure they are tapping into all the available talent. A CEO of one of our member companies likens this to putting together a football team. You wouldn't just pick from half the roster to make your starting team.

I also believe it's important that we NOT position this as women vs. men. As I've listened to stories from women and men around the world, I've come to one overwhelming conclusion. There's no such thing as men leaders and women leaders—there are only good leaders and bad leaders. Some of them are men, and some of them are women.

True leadership is not a function of authority, but of behavior. The best leaders cultivate the traits that Catalyst research links to inclusion. (We refer to these by the acronym EACH.)

- **E**mpowerment: Empowering team members to succeed
- **A**ccountability: Holding team members accountable for their work
- **C**ourage: Courageously taking risks to uphold their principles
- **H**umility: Being humble enough to admit mistakes and learn from different points of view

In our report on inclusive leadership, we found that managers who were perceived to exhibit these EACH behaviors have direct reports who feel more included by virtue of experiencing a greater sense of belonging and uniqueness within their respective work-groups. We also found that the more included employees felt, the more they reported proposing new ideas and engaging in group citizenship and teamwork. At Catalyst, we have a handy quiz—called "Are You an Inclusive Leader?"—which helps managers determine whether they are leading with an inclusive mind-set.

What are the major obstacles that hinder women from attaining decision-making posts?

While women have made great strides in recent decades, they still face barriers to success in the corporate world today. But these barriers are more often the result of unconscious biases and assumptions about women's skills and aspirations—rather than overt sexism. Even well intended leaders who believe in gender equality can have biases that can hold women back.

Our research also shows that women often lack access to influential sponsors and hot jobs—those highly visible, mission-critical roles that predict advancement.

Our research also shows that women often lack access to influential sponsors and hot jobs—those highly visible, mission-critical roles that predict advancement, such as international assignments, profit-and-loss and budget responsibility, and management of large teams.

How can we overcome the obstacles?

This isn't about fixing women. It's about fixing the barriers that are happening in the workplace. Consciously practicing the inclusive leadership skills I mentioned earlier can go a long way toward rooting out the biases that hold women back today.

- **Inclusive leaders make an intentional effort to avoid being blinded by stereotypes.** They identify people's strengths, show them what's possible, and commit to helping them get there.

- **Inclusive leaders avoid assumptions.** Never assume a women with children wouldn't be interested in a high-profile assignment or relocating for an exciting new role—ask her!

- **Inclusive leadership means stepping up or speaking up, when remaining silent is easier or safer.** If you walk into a department meeting or board room and see only men, ask why. Each and every one of us has the potential to step up and become a leader for the world of today, making a deliberate choice to disrupt the status quo.

Here are some **other strategies** that Catalyst recommends for making significant change.

Tone from the top is key. Leaders must be fully committed to creating a workplace where women and men can be equally successful, to designing strategies for getting there, and to holding leaders accountable for meeting goals along the way.

> Leaders must be fully committed to creating a workplace where women and men can be equally successful.

There must be a clearly defined business rationale for why it is necessary to focus on women, and it must be consistently reinforced in the organization. We see this happening with our Catalyst Award–winning companies and leaders, who are making great progress toward achieving more inclusive workplaces where woman and men can advance and thrive. They are instituting policies, programs, and initiatives to ensure that all talent will have the opportunity to contribute and succeed. They are raising awareness of unconscious bias and stereotypes through training for leaders/managers, and they are creating networks and opportunities for women to connect with other leaders and other women in their organizations.

Involve individuals across all levels of an organization. Though essential, the top-down approach alone is not enough. Changing policies and creating programs is not enough. It takes individuals across all levels to shift mind-sets and behaviors so that women receive the support they need to rise up through the ranks. Companies don't make change, people do—reaching those in middle management is essential.

Catalyst's research on inclusive leadership and our learning programs/partnerships with edX (nonprofit online initiative created by founding partners at Harvard and MIT) and Blessing White (global consulting firm dedicated to leadership development and employee engagement) are getting at that group of middle managers who are eager to learn how to best support their employees and help them succeed and advance. Around 60,000 people from 200 countries have taken part in our online training courses with 60 percent of them men!

> We often hear about the importance of having mentors, but sponsors are critical for advancement.

Sponsorship. We often hear about the importance of having mentors, but sponsors are critical for advancement. What's the difference? A mentor will talk with you, offering advice. Sponsors—influential senior leaders—talk *about* you, and advocate for you at the decision-making table, which is critical when promotions or other opportunities are being discussed. At virtually every stage of my career, I've benefitted from that kind of sponsorship. I had sponsors who were prepared to say,

"This is the right opportunity for Deborah, and she is ready. We really should invest in her success."

Since men are still in the majority of leadership positions, they are essential to driving change.

Engage men in change: Since men are still in the majority of leadership positions, they are essential to driving change. In trying to help his leadership team understand the importance and benefits of sponsorship, the CEO of one of our Catalyst Award–winning companies recounted how he asked them to write down the names of the three people who had made a difference in their careers. Then, he asked them to write down the names of the three people who would put them on their list if he asked them the same question. Last, he asked them to consider whether everyone on their list looked just like them. It's really important for organizations and their leaders to remember the benefits of sponsorship in their own careers, and then to make sure that they are not just sponsoring other males, but women too.

It's time to redefine leadership for today's working world and build workforces and leadership teams that look like the communities we serve. That means building inclusive workplaces where women and men are given equal chances to succeed—and equal pay for equal work.

7

Improving the Place
of Women in the Economy

INTERVIEW WITH AUDRA BOHANNON, SENIOR PARTNER AT KORN FERRY'S LEADERSHIP AND TALENT CONSULTING

Leadership is not gender specific.

What place do women occupy in the economic world—both as employees and entrepreneurs—in the United States or globally today?

They represent a huge economic opportunity, and we should expect from women what we expect from men—to be highly engaged, strong contributors, great managers, and effective leaders. If you look at the number of women active in the workforce, and the contributions we've made, and when you think that most small businesses, especially in the United States, are started and run by women, women are a huge power and a huge force.

What assets do women managers and women entrepreneurs have?

As little girls, women are raised to support, nurture, and care-take as well as engage in high achievement. This places women in an enviable position. As they continue to take on higher-level roles, they can bring a level of compassion, support, and care to their organizations. Women do not tend to be command and control; they do not tend to be "it's just about me." They bring consensus building and collaboration, as well as making an impact and getting results. Women bring perspective, skills, attitudes, and expertise that can significantly improve how we can move forward as a society.

What female stereotypes still prevail in our society? What are the major obstacles that hinder women from attaining decision-making posts?

The prevailing stereotypes are that women are too emotional and too soft to make the tough, hard decisions that come with leadership. There is this notion that women are hard workers—they get the job done and done well. We think tactically and not strategically, and tend to be seen more on the execution side of the equation and not on the side of strategy and leadership.

Are certain sectors more favorable to women than others? Do women do well in them?

Sectors that allow flexibility with work schedules and are more focused on deliverables than "face time" draw women their way (e.g., IT, professional services, etc.). The STEM areas—Science, Technology, Engineering, and Mathematics—offer significant upside for women. However, there is still so much work to be done since, in most organizations, whether it's for profit or nonprofit, when you look at where women sit, they are usually below director level and when you look at who sits at director level and above, it's predominantly white men.

What are the keys to improving the place of women in the economy?

Sponsorship, mentoring, advocacy, and support. In the United States, there was a survey to assess what are the critical requirements to increase the number of girls who decided to go into STEM areas. One key factor was having a role model. They said that it's important for little girls to see themselves in key roles thinking, "If she can do it, then I can too." Also many articles have been published about the criticality of women having support from individuals who are willing to invest in their futures. Without key relationships of influence, it is hard to move strategically within an organization. If organizations want to retain a significant part of the workforce, that is, women, they need to consistently provide guidance, coaching, mentoring, and sponsorship for women just as they do for men. Help them to navigate—understand when to go to the right, when to go to the left, when to stop and when to start, when to speed up and when to slow down. We all have blind spots, so having a community of support, where others help you "see" and position you for expanded responsibilities, is vital. Women should seek these critical resources and the organization should provide them.

But, there are some personal challenges women themselves face. Women work hard every day managing the personal and professional sides of their lives. They manage their time as efficiently as they can. So when they think about what's required to build the quality of relationships and networks to drive their careers, the question can be "Do I have the time?" Messages received when we were little girls can also slow women's career progression. Trying to manage it all can sometimes create ambivalence. And finally there is the whole guilt thing: women talk about how, on Sunday evenings, they're tied up in knots, because they're thinking about work but they should be at home, so it's like, "I'm damned if I do, I'm damned if I don't."

Ambivalence, guilt, and not understanding and investing in the relationship are examples of factors that can slow women down and/or compromise their vision. By seeing most challenges as influence situations, they could move into a problem-solving orientation and find a solution to address the outcome they seek.

Does the new economy, in particular, the social enterprise aspects of the new economy, give women the opportunity to develop their presence?

Absolutely, not only their presence but also their leadership. There are two things that are happening: health care in the United States is going through an overhaul, technology has removed the borders, and we are a global economy. We don't have enough doctors or nurses to be able to take care of everyone; baby boomers, a significant force, are getting older and will need more medical attention. If women are in health care right now, the opportunities to lead and engineer a career will be available to them. In our global economy, the more we are relevant and efficient in achieving the goals and objectives of our organizations, the more flexibility and mobility there will be for women.

It is a wonderful time for being a woman in this world of ours—we've hit a tipping point; it is our moment in time. It's now about choices women can make in support of living fulfilling lives based on their own definition of success. Organizations as well need to continue to commit to building cultures that demonstrate appreciation of women.

Leadership is not gender specific. Women and men can lead. In terms of driving change, having significant impact, running an organization or country, with the strong support of mentoring, advocacy, and sponsorship, women can do as well as and maybe even better than men. I fundamentally believe that with all my heart.

History will write a chapter about life during our times. What will it say about the commitment on the part of organizations to really see women as the valuable assets they are? If companies fully embrace what women can do and provide the critical mentoring/advocacy/sponsorship support, we will see women proportionately represented at all levels in an organization. Women as well should mentor and support each other so that in the end the chapter is written and written well about the significant contributions made by women and the difference they made in shaping our society.

8

Overcoming Women's Obstacles

INTERVIEW WITH CHRISTIANE BERGEVIN, EXECUTIVE VICE PRESIDENT AT DESJARDINS GROUP

Women have to network a lot more and a lot earlier.

How do you see the role of women in today's economic/financial world?

Twofold—there's a huge number of extremely qualified women, and there's a great complementarity when women achieve executive roles in sufficient numbers. If you compare it with a sports team, your bench is bigger if you have more skill sets. So for a company, when you have a big bench of competent, qualified people, you're just better off.

In Canada there are women at the top, and their thinking process is slightly different—and it's highly complementary with men. It's like in a couple: if you have just one person making the decisions, it lacks complementarity. Women in the economic and financial world should be in significant numbers, so that companies can make use of all the players on the bench. University provides a bench of players, and then it's the role of organizations to develop those players, just the way a professional sports team develops its players. This means that eventually, all those seated on that bench can be called to be the next captain. And then you have not only a broader bench and a broader skill set, but it's highly complementary.

Do you think women managers bring any particular advantages to the company?

I think each gender brings specific skills — not only for women, but for men as well. We cannot make this a general statement, but quite often women will be more intuitive, will be very good at thinking out of the box and, very importantly, also very good at reading personalities.

> Quite often women will be more intuitive, will be very good at thinking out of the box and, very importantly, also very good at reading personalities.

I'd say that guys also have their skills — they often sell better, they're more confident about their own skill set, they're ready to be CEO of a major company and they've not even been an executive! Whereas women say, "Whoah, I'm not sure." Guys will be more, perhaps, bold — not that there aren't women who are bold — but guys are bolder in general — but women are very good at understanding the human character, which is, after all, what the service industry consists of.

What are the major obstacles that prevent women from attaining key decision-making posts?

Money, power, and influence.

Money: If you look at the HR department, women do pretty well. They're at the top. But in a major company, your profit center is usually where remuneration is the highest, and in your support sectors, remuneration is not at the same level.

So why do women do very well in HR positions—including being at the top? Why is it that they achieve that status without any issue? At SNC-Lavalin Capital, in that project finance environment where I worked before, we had the highest paid staff of all the Canadian market, but why was that? It's because in an investment bank, if you make money, you create greater competition, and that creates greater recruitment—"I'll hire you, I know you—you're good." But in that element, women often lose because the team go for drinks after work—but women don't have time because they have kids. So the proximity, the network, is not there.

Power: Look at any management team, and there are some women—but in a minority—and the contribution of the person in the minority tends to be excluded. I sit in my organization, sit around the table, and we have a CEO who's a woman. She has changed many dimensions—she has brought many more women, and so suddenly we have many more women in the executive ranks. Now will this last when she goes? I doubt it because the power circle tends to stick to the male group.

Influence: It's the same thing. For me, the role of money, power, and influence tends to be highly protected within male circles.

How can we help women to overcome these obstacles?

There should be no bias—but I think there is this stigma, this bias. In terms of gender, you can't have blind interviews the way they did with the studies on recruitment of violinists. There's always bias in recruitment.

> Women have to network a lot more and a lot earlier ... act as if there were no barriers.

In the Top 100 Women interview that I did, I said there are two elements: first, women have to network a lot more and a lot earlier. At school you'll be the best if you get the best marks, and you'll get the best marks if you study more or if you're bright. But that's not enough in a work environment because some people who are mediocre or average get to the top. So it comes down to networking—networking is important, and you need to invest in it earlier. But not just networking between women.

The second thing is: act as if there were no barriers. Because there are barriers to overcome, and it's difficult, but in a sense, just act as if there were no barriers. And most importantly, invest in a skill set that's also very good. Invest in anticipation. Networking is key, but anticipation is even more important. What are the differences between the best tennis players? What makes one better than the others? They're faster. Why are they faster? They anticipate the intention of the other player better. Roger Federer moves faster; Martina Navratilova moves faster, and if you're ready, if you're already there when the ball gets to you because you've anticipated, then it's easy to hit the ball. Anticipation means building a better strategy.

I think it's the role of each woman executive—this is my final point—to create, to support, to—I don't like the word "mentor" because I think it's like an inferior person seeking help—but to advise, to meet, and to convey your experience as the more senior person—provide little pieces of encouragement, of advice, that will make the younger person progress faster.

Do you have a mentoring program in Desjardins?

I prefer the term "coaching" by the way. The reason I don't like "mentoring" is because a guy, an experienced director, will mentor women. And this looks kind of second class to me, whereas anyone who wants to be on the board should be mentored. But the word gets used so much in male/female contexts where the female is the junior. You don't think about mentoring for a guy—you think about a sponsor or a coach, but not a mentor. So "mentor" brings a connotation that a woman needs a mentor, and a guy needs a sponsor.

I'm a strong sponsor and a strong coach outside and inside the organization. I try to give back as much as I can within the time limits—giving the tips, pushing someone, saying, "Hey gee, you can get on the board, you need to be on the board," and I see them a year after and they say, "Well, you know I thought about it, and I joined one"—so it's helping.

I think we each have a role to play and a large number of men are also ready to do so. We do it in Quebec perhaps more than elsewhere in Canada because there's a differentiating factor for Quebec: there are more women CEOs than anywhere else in the country, because we've had a program of equal representation on boards that are owned by the Government, such as the Liquor Board. It's the first place in North America and the second place in the world after Norway. This initiative has paid off a lot; for example, as part of that program, I was named on the board of a pension fund—a $200 billion pension fund—and I might never have been on that board because the Chair, when I met him, said, "Oh you're the age of my daughter." But I was obviously qualified, I had a finance background, and I'd made my mark, but because of his attitude, I might not have gotten onto the board. I'd say that the governor of Quebec has invested in something that is equally if not more important than coaching: he has invested in creating equal access for women.

9

Women's Spirit of Enterprise

INTERVIEW WITH VALÉRIE BERNIS, EXECUTIVE VICE PRESIDENT AT ENGIE, IN CHARGE OF COMMUNICATIONS, MARKETING, AND ENVIRONMENTAL AND SOCIETAL RESPONSIBILITY

> We are living in ... a world undergoing profound changes, which requires greater agility, daring, and cohesion. I am convinced that women have a decisive role to play here.

Valérie Bernis was a staff member at the French Ministry of Economy, Finance and Privatization (1986–1988), and later in charge of communications and the press on the staff of the French prime minister (1993–1995). She joined SUEZ in 1996 and in 1999 became a member of its Executive Committee, in charge of Communications, Financial Communications, and Sustainable Development. At the same time, she was chairman and CEO of Paris Première and a board member of several international companies. She is a member of the Euro Disney Supervisory

Board and the boards of directors of SUEZ Environnement, Atos, Occitane, and AROP Association pour le Rayonnement de l'Opéra National de Paris (Paris Opera supporting association).

As Gérard Mestrallet, chairman of ENGIE, was aware of Valérie Bernis's commitment to the place of women in the company, in 2007 he gave her the responsibility of considering the topic at length and producing an action plan.

Since May 1, 2011, Valérie Bernis has been a member of the ENGIE Executive Committee and executive vice president of the company.

In your experience as a top-level manager, do you think that there are differences in the way men and women achieve such senior roles?

Let us share the following observation: today in 2016 women still have difficulty in asserting their leadership in an environment that continues to promote traditionally a mainly male managerial model. A large number of women regularly tell me that they are not at ease with the notion of power, with asserting their ambitions, with promoting their successes, or even with negotiating their salary.

Many of them make the choice of moving to roles as specialists or experts, rather than take up more visible roles in management. This is at the risk of being confined to very support roles that do not give the necessary visibility for them to develop their talent.

Inside ENGIE, we have already provided several answers to that observation: the Mentoring by ENGIE program aimed at high-potential women; Taking the Stage, an awareness-creation tool developed by a Canadian agency for 1,800 women in the Group's international women's network (WIN: Women In Networking); and the development of an "Experts" activity line that helps identify the Group's future senior executives within that talent pool.

In 2013, we decided to go a step further by launching a program devoted to leadership for all women in ENGIE, both managers and those destined to carry out managerial responsibilities. The program aims at giving women the keys for exercising power, for removing their blind spots, and for developing their rightful ambitions.

It is a real tool for strengthening female leadership on a large scale, in line with the demands for adapting to the economic and social world, which is encouraging a greater diversity of leaders.

The same question regarding your experience as a member of boards of directors

I am delighted to see the major projects that have been carried out over the past few years in increasing the number of women on Boards of Directors, especially in France.

When I took on my first board duties in the 1990s, very few women were members of those bodies, and I can remember the debates that took place over the enactment of the Copé-Zimmerman Act, which, in France, introduced representative quotas of each gender for listed companies. Since so few women were board members, how could we possibly promote female career profiles—was this not a sign that women were not interested in those responsibilities?

We have to admit that the act pushed boundaries very quickly. And very talented and able women were ready for board mandates. Without this bill, they probably would never have gained access to these responsibilities. Women now bring all their know-how and skills to company boards. More than simply gender equality, it is a guarantee of performance and efficiency, of a complementary point of view that enhances company governance.

So I am particularly proud that following the voting at ENGIE's Mixed General Shareholders' on April 28, 2015, the Group's Board of Directors now has 63 percent women, the most female-representative board in the CAC 40.

You have a cultural and family background that is very entrepreneurial. Has this entrepreneurial spirit helped you to succeed? Do you think that this spirit of entrepreneurship/intrapreneurship can help women to succeed?

I believe in businesses, whatever their size.

Businesses are examples of the most fantastic human adventures, and the wealth they produce is not just financial.

As I am from a family of entrepreneurs, I understood very early in my life what a mine of initiative, resoluteness, effort, patience, and determination hid behind the word "entrepreneur." Its qualities, which were decisive in my career path, seem to me to be even more vital in the world we are living in, a world undergoing profound changes, which requires greater agility, daring, and cohesion. I am convinced that women have a decisive role to play here.

At ENGIE, we can see that momentum—women's spirit of enterprise—in numerous initiatives that we are backing. Outside the group, we are signed up to initiatives that support women's startups and SMEs (small and medium-sized enterprises). In 2014, we launched an incubation organization for employees to develop their projects in an adapted and safe framework. In particular, the incubator helped us to support new business projects—including some really remarkable ones—proposed by women from ENGIE's Women In Networking network, each one sponsored by one of the group's executive vice presidents.

In your opinion, are mentoring and sponsorship complementary in the workplace? How can these two levers be used in the most effective way?

Since 2008, as executive vice president, I have stimulated and supported ENGIE's commitment to the place of women in the company. Through program after program, we have carried out experiments, run pilots, and built up best practices in order to achieve ambitious goals and produce sustainable tools.

One of those tools—mentoring—stands out, with at least three virtues: helping mentees achieve their goals, including, but not only, top management posts; establishing mentors firmly in their responsibility; and proving that not only human beings, but also human relationships, have their place at the heart of the company—and even that those relationships are a criterion of performance.

In 2015, no technology or algorithm contributed more to that than the eyes of others: vigilant and kind eyes, eyes that encompass a wide view, knowing eyes. Basically, that is what a mentor represents, at any rate the mentors I know and the mentor that I hope I am. Questions from mentees often bring mentors back to their past experiences but also make them think about their future.

Mentoring is a three-sided story: mentor, mentee, and company. It is a win-win-win program, enabling people to work on mentalities, creating a snowball effect that goes beyond the players concerned.

As well as mentoring, I also recommend that women develop their networks, build relationships of trust around them, and publicize their successes and their ambitions. That is how they will rally allies around them, true sponsors who believe in their potential and will act as facilitators whenever opportunities present themselves, as career accelerators.

Sponsors and mentors take part in a complementary approach, which is absolutely vital for career paths.

Statistics aside, have you noticed a change in the way in which the men in the group regard the careers of women?

Absolutely.

Let's face it, we are in the midst of the technological and economic upheavals to come. This period is challenging for us: we are not just going through one crisis, nor several crises—we are undergoing profound changes.

We can choose to hold on to our entrenched positions, our exclusive preserve, our acquired assets. Or we can choose to move forward and embrace the unknown. To endure changes or to take part in them. We must be even bolder, even more courageous, and even more tenacious. We must give up on giving up. We have "to dare to dare."

Daring is what we showed in 2008, when our chairman, Gérard Mestrallet, spurred on our full policy in favor of the place of women. It was a visionary and brave initiative, a strong signal to our entire company.

This ambitious policy, the mentoring program in particular, has truly changed mentalities and helped to establish a real culture of gender diversity. By involving male mentors, we have created a genuine new awareness.

As we have always stated, we cannot advance the place of women without the commitment of everyone, men and women. It is not simply a question of equality, but a challenge to society, a question of performance for our organizations. I believe that this message is truly a shared one, that depriving ourselves of one-half of human talent is, quite frankly, inept.

Gender equality is the key to the future — a key to performance — in all aspects of our lives, particularly in companies.

Part III

DESIGNING MENTORING AND SPONSORING PROGRAMS

IN TODAY'S WORLD, EVERY MAJOR GROUP is aware of the gender gap, and significant progress has been made to narrow it through programs to support and promote women at all levels of management. Mentoring and sponsoring are key tools in these programs.

But for mentoring and sponsoring to be successful, they need to be recognized as key to achieving the company's aims—integrating employees and engaging them with the company's values—and they need to be implemented throughout the workforce, and supported by CEOs.

Gérard Mestrallet (chairman of ENGIE) points to studies showing that gender equality and diversity increase the company's overall performance, and while he recognizes that the bottom line is important, he also believes that major groups should be leading social thinking and social change. For ENGIE, the aim is to recruit not only a good mix of men and women, as well as a mix of talents, but to ensure that this mix is mirrored at managerial level and board level. In 2008 ENGIE set up its Women In Networking program, aimed at increasing women's visibility in the group, and then, in 2010, launched the Mentoring at ENGIE program specifically designed to help women to break through the glass ceiling to positions of key responsibility. For mentoring and sponsoring to be successful, men too need to engage with it, not only to understand the aspirations and obstacles faced by high-potential women, but to recognize mentoring as a way to understand the company in its fast-changing environment.

Leopoldo Boado (chairman of Oracle Spain) also points to the tangible benefits of mentoring, and sees mentoring and sponsoring programs as both a talent retention tool and a talent management tool that develops internal talent and gives the company a global competitive advantage. Oracle is the pioneer of cross-company mentoring, pairing mentors and mentees of different companies, enabling mentees to develop their skills, and mentors to develop their leadership capabilities. As Leopoldo points out, mentoring is an "initiative that aligns equitable treatment and talent development."

For Maurice Levy (chairman of Publicis Groupe), mentoring requires confidentiality, and so mentoring pairs never come from the same subsidiary. For him, the mentoring program VivaWomen!—which is implemented through either mentoring circles or mentoring pairs—is designed to develop talented women and enable them to fulfill their ambitions. The benefits that flow from this are stronger internal relationships and teams, more effective management, and greater confidence in relationships with clients. Again, this improves overall performance and effective talent retention.

BNP Paribas runs a range of mentoring programs, which are designed to complement the bank's Management Academy, where employees can develop their skills and professional expertise. According to Marie-Claire Capobianco, head of Retail Banking at BNP Paribas, mentoring "adds knowledge and understanding to the whole professional landscape," and enables mentees to realize the full range of their capabilities. Mentoring at BNP Paribas is only one of a range of measures the bank employs in its commitment to equality: these include agreements signed with the United Nations and the French Ministry of Women's Rights, an internal network of women managers to provide support, the signing of the Parents' Charter, and the setting up of a Diversity Committee to monitor recruitment and career development.

And at BNY Mellon, Karen Peetz (president) is passionate about equality and diversity. She suggests that lack of sponsors and lack of role models are the main obstacles that stand in the way of women's success—closely followed by others' prejudices as well as women's own limited horizons. At BNY Mellon, Karen and her teams have implemented a range of measures to ensure equal opportunity—and equal possibilities to seize those opportunities. These include employee resources groups, which are structured networks where people can gain exposure, professional development, and business experience; the "Nine Box Talent Review," which requires every name in the team to be considered for promotion; and Reverse Mentoring, which connects senior people with junior people for mutual benefit: the juniors gain exposure to wisdom and experience, while the seniors get to hear the views of recent recruits and what management should be doing to address their concerns. BNY Mellon has seen a 100 percent increase in the number of women in the workforce, with 36 percent of women at the VP level, 26 percent at the MD level, and 19 percent of the Board of Directors are women.

Part III explains in some detail how to set up a mentoring or sponsoring program: the aims, the various structures, the outcomes, and the benefits in terms of performance, management effectiveness, team leadership and participation, corporate identity, and talent development and retention.

The keys to success are often the willingness of a manager, or group of managers, and the resources invested in achieving the goals.

Mentoring should not be improvised, but rather prepared and believed in throughout the company—and supported by both women and men.

Mentoring programs must be structured, open to everyone, trackable, and sustainable. Mentoring is not a passing fancy, but a means to promotion and equality, which the CEO needs to support continuously.

10

"Mentoring by ENGIE"

INTERVIEW WITH GÉRARD MESTRALLET, CHAIRMAN OF ENGIE

Why has ENGIE implemented a mentoring program aimed at women?

It's my belief that our group, that every group, should not only mirror society but lead social change and social thinking. To develop gender diversity requires daring, courage, and a certain level of determination. These are values that our group nurtures and wants our female employees to contribute to, and developing these values is in our interest, in the interest of our women, and in the interest of our men. Studies demonstrate that gender diversity and equality of opportunity can increase our overall performance as a company. In order to succeed in achieving these ends, we not only need a solid strategy but also to recruit a good mix of men and women, and a mix of different talents, but also to appoint a similar mix in our managers, and to elect such a mix to our board of directors. Of course, there are still cultural and historical difficulties, and this is why, with Valérie Bernis, ENGIE executive vice president, we agreed, in 2008, to an ambitious and global policy aimed at supporting and promoting women throughout the group. In 2008, we also launched a program called Women In Networking (WIN), an international network of ENGIE women whose goal is to help women throughout the group become stronger and more visible. Then, in 2010, when we became aware of the fact that women encounter difficulties to break through the glass ceiling and access more senior positions, we launched the program Mentoring at ENGIE. This program, specifically designed to respond to women and their aspirations, provides structures and/or mentors to support their professional development. The program has been welcomed by our male employees and by senior managers who have accepted the challenge and proved themselves excellent and engaged mentors.

What can we learn from this program, and what are the outcomes?

What we've noticed, now that the third round of mentoring has finished, is that mentoring has been an incredible way to build employees' self-confidence and to introduce different perspectives—the two, of course, being closely linked. Each mentee has been able to reflect on her role, and, thanks to her mentor, to develop her career. The rate of satisfaction is very high (close to 100 percent), both on the part of mentees as well as mentors. It's important to underline this, since mentoring not only benefits the mentees, but it also provides great benefits to the mentors. Our mentors are senior executives who can, through mentoring, understand more clearly the aspirations of our high-potential women, and develop their skills. For both sets of participants, mentoring is also a way to discover and understand the group, something that is essential in our current and changing business environment.

What would you like to see happen after this experience?

In addition to the very positive impact on women in our group, the success of our first three rounds of the mentoring program has also enabled us to establish mentoring as a key part of the group's culture, and to include it in our management style. With the support of the Steering Committee, we decided to extend the program and, in spring 2014, we launched a global mentoring initiative, which aims to mentor a thousand young managers—both men and women—from all business sectors of the group. As far as young, high-potential women are concerned, round four of the ENGIE mentoring program was launched at the end of 2014 with a strengthened international dimension. I am keen that we continue with our initial goal: to develop mentalities, and change opinions on gender diversity and equality of opportunity: it's the essence of WIN, the goal of mentoring, and the reason behind every action we've undertaken since 2008. Thanks to this remarkable movement of men and women, the ENGIE group is particularly well-positioned in this important arena of gender diversity, and we will continue to develop and to implement concrete actions to support women in our group: it's in the interest of all of us.

"MENTORING BY ENGIE," A STRUCTURED PROGRAM TO TRAIN WOMEN AS LEADERS

The Mentoring Program at ENGIE

Aims

Career development; facilitation of women's access to senior posts.

Program Details and Aims

Women In Networking (WIN): to develop careers and achieve gender diversity.

Mentoring at ENGIE: to improve high-potential women's access to senior posts.

Outcomes

For mentees: objectives met, company loyalty and retention, pride in the company, understanding of how the company

(continued)

(continued)

works, acquisition of tools and good practices; 37 percent
of mentees promoted, increase in role models, increase in
responsibilities.
For mentors: awareness of obstacles to women's career progression and the levers that help, improvement in managerial skills,
reassessment of own careers and career paths.

Since 2008, ENGIE has run a number of programs aimed at
women. The aim of all these programs is to support women's
career development within the group and, more broadly, to
support a culture of diversity. It's in this framework that, in
September 2008, the WIN (Women In Networking) network
was launched. In January 2010, encouraged by the success of
WIN, ENGIE launched its first mentoring program aimed at
connecting high-potential women with the group's directors or
senior management in order to improve women's access to senior
posts. Before running this program on a larger scale, ENGIE first
of all launched it as a pilot to test and fine-tune the idea.

Content, Issues, and Aims

When they hit the glass ceiling, high-potential women in ENGIE
were either not breaking through or were leaving the group.
To rectify this situation, ENGIE's one-year mentoring program
addressed a number of issues:

- To mark the group's commitment to women
- To highlight women's talents internally
- To achieve more women directors and senior managers
- To involve both men and women in gender diversity

Mentoring is based on a culture of generosity, respect, and
sharing. Helping mentees to develop requires the achievement of
several goals determined by the mentor and the mentee. Their
relationship is based on mutual exchange.

FOR THE MENTEE, THE ADVANTAGES ARE

- Learning to "decode" how the company works by learning from the experience of a colleague within the group
- Receiving advice on career choices and career path
- Receiving support to take on a director or senior management–level post
- Developing knowledge and networks

FOR THE MENTOR, THE ADVANTAGES ARE

- Becoming aware of, and making others aware of, the challenges that women face
- Being enriched by the relationship with another person (the mentee)
- Strengthening internal cohesion

Keys to Success

For the mentoring program to succeed, it needed mutual trust, confidentiality, integrity, honesty, professionalism, rigor, and respect for diversity. In addition to these values, certain rules were established to ensure the program's success. These included: having the mentor and mentee come from different departments, clearly defined objectives from the beginning, equal involvement in the relationship, regular meetings, confidentiality, defined parameters to frame the relationship (e.g., career development), rigorous follow-up of the mentoring by the program team, and problem-solving processes in case of difficulties in the relationship.

Program and Selection

In order to have a representative sample for the pilot, ENGIE set up 45 mentoring pairs. The mentees selected were high-potential women and members of the WIN network. As for mentors, they were more experienced males and females at director or senior management level, with no direct line management to the mentee, who could help their mentees to progress via their experience and their networks.

For the selection process, all candidates wrote a paper explaining why they were motivated to join the program, and detailed topics they wished to discuss. The mentors were chosen mainly for their commitment to gender diversity, but they also had to be able to give constructive feedback; be open-minded, patient, attentive, and tolerant; have a strategic vision of the company; display leadership qualities; and know how to take a step back and evaluate the mentee's progress. As for the mentees, they had to be motivated to progress and break through career steps, eager to understand and analyze their strengths and the possible obstacles hindering their progression, open to another's point of view, and able to hear other people's advice. They were selected on the basis of an analysis of their motivation to be mentored, and then by a matching of their needs with the areas offered by the mentors.

Preparation of the Participants

A key factor in the success of the mentoring program was the very detailed and thorough preparation of the mentors and mentees. The mentors followed three collective training sessions. First session: stages of the pilot program, mentor behavior, application, mentoring tools (arbitrage, self governance, positioning, etc.), semantics, and ethics. At the end of this session the pairs met each other for a first "get to know you" session. Second session: the mentors were provided with additional tools and reading on behavior and attitudes. Third and final session: how to adjust to the mentoring situation. Finally, an individual coaching session enabled the mentors to prepare for their mentoring relationship.

The mentees participated in a session to prepare them for meeting their respective mentors. At the end of this session, they had a good idea of the objectives and limits of the program, their roles as mentees, and the steps in the mentoring relationship.

Animation and Follow-Up

The relationship between the mentor and mentee, key to the success of the program, required monitoring to avoid any potential difficulties. To do this, the quality of the mentoring relationship was assessed via a questionnaire from the beginning of the program. This meant that any readjustments could be quickly made in case of problems. Then two meetings were scheduled to follow up the development of the mentoring relationship. The mentees were able to share their experiences, exchange good practices, and learn how to revitalize their relationship if needed. Finally some benefited from an individual follow-up to adjust the mentoring pair, especially when the pair lacked dynamism.

Feedback

To assess the success of the program, each participant was asked to complete a questionnaire, and the mentees were also interviewed. This showed that the mentoring relationship was seen as serious (98 percent satisfaction rate by mentors and mentees); 84 percent of mentees and 91 percent of mentors thought the objectives had been achieved and that the mentors paid attention to the quality of the discussions. Meetings to put issues into perspective were considered useful by 60 percent of the mentees, with comments that these meetings allowed them to take some distance and to share their experiences. The mentors thought the training was useful (96 percent) and necessary to understand their role and acquire mentoring expertise. The program's virtuous circle had, in addition, strengthened mentees' loyalty and increased their pride in the company. As for the mentors, they had become more aware of the issues, problems, and levers helping and hindering women's career progression in the company.

Outcomes

Thanks to the mentoring program, the mentees were able to continue the work themselves and become aware of their positioning in the company. Other benefits included an understanding of the company and the way it worked, the ability to put things into perspective, and the acquisition of tools and good practices. At the end of the program, 37 percent of mentees progressed in their careers; some changed their posts and took on more responsibilities, while others became role models in their departments. The mentors acquired mentoring skills and strengthened their managerial abilities. Some even re-assessed their own career progression! Their discussions with the mentees in effect made them look at their own pasts and futures.

The program was run again in March 2012 with 61 mentoring pairs of whom 8 were international, then again in Autumn 2013 and by the end of 2014. The second and third mentoring seasons confirmed the considerable impact the program has had on the mentees' career development and the awareness of directors and senior managers around the issues of gender diversity.

Finally, the program was transformational within ENGIE, not only for the mentors and mentees, but for all colleagues. Mentoring has led to a change in mind-sets by creating a snowball effect, which has moved quickly beyond the players immediately involved in the program. This virtuous circle has generated a positive image on the Internet, and mentalities have changed, with more men now aware of women as leaders.

11

Oracle Women Leadership (OWL) Mentoring Program

INTERVIEW WITH LEOPOLDO BOADO, CHAIRMAN OF ORACLE SPAIN

Why has Oracle Spain implemented a mentoring program?

At Oracle, we foster an inclusive and innovative environment that leverages the gender, diversity, backgrounds, and perspectives of our employees, customers, suppliers, and partners to drive a global competitive advantage. And to be successful, we also need to develop, engage, and empower current and future Oracle generations based on integrity and equity.

Mentoring allows us to develop our internal talent and learn to think in a different way, outside of our comfort zone. It is a powerful talent management tool that helps to develop our people.

Our mentees are Top Talents (men and especially women) with potential but with developmental needs; this program enables them to accelerate their professional growth and also enables the mentors to continuously develop their leadership skills. There is a very special focus on women to help them to solve any social or career barriers to develop their potential.

We have different initiatives, like some mentoring programs under the Spanish Equity projects (especially OWL), or the Cross Company Mentoring, which is a program that introduces a new way to share the company's best practices. It is an initiative that aligns equitable treatment and talent development, combining internal and external requirements.

What can we learn from this program, and what are the outcomes?

The program gives the opportunity to learn from professionals of a high level in another business, applicable to both mentors and mentees. The mentees are able to develop their skills supported by leaders of different areas and, in parallel, the mentors develop their leadership capabilities too, outside their daily scope.

Through this program, the mentors should enable mentees to learn from their past successes and failures, and encourage them to engage in self-determined learning and to find their own solutions. We receive very good feedback from all the participants.

Regarding Cross Company mentoring, we have been pioneers in creating this mentoring model, being a reference for other companies in Spain.

What would you like to see happen after this experience?

Oracle employees get a further and faster development, getting a better gender equity balance in managerial positions and readiness to assume new responsibilities. It is also key for spreading the network and enhancing collaboration.

I would like to continue with this program, in order to create a strong and diverse leadership organization, which will lead to success in the IT market.

As a summary, developing and retaining our top talents and achieving a gender equity balance are key objectives for Oracle Spain and the Country Leadership Team. We are sure that it makes us a high potential organization.

ORACLE'S MENTORING PROGRAM AND INTERCOMPANY EXPERIENCE

The Mentoring Program at Oracle

Aims

Increase number of women in management roles; increase recruitment of women generally

Program Details and Aims

Diversity and Equality program: increase diversity and equality of opportunity

Oracle Women Leadership (OWL) and mentoring program: increase number of women leaders

Outcomes

Development of networks, enhancement of professional and individual profiles, new perspectives on working, promotion of corporate values

The computer giant, Oracle, wants to increase the number of women in management roles and in strategic programs. Consequently, it is implementing a gender and diversity policy to increase the proportion of women in the IT world, which has witnessed a substantial decrease over several years. Oracle has therefore launched a European-level project called "Diversity and Equality."

The desire to turn these proportions around can be clearly seen in the readjustment of salaries between men and women, which Oracle has been working on for three years in Europe. Another area for improvement is recruitment: from now on the company intends to have at least one woman in every short list for jobs, and if there is no woman, the recruiters must explain why not. Various measures will also be used to alert managers in charge of promotions, appraisals, and salary increases to any imbalances or gaps experienced by women. In addition, the HR Department organizes regular sessions to inform managers about the performance of mixed-gender teams.

Aims, Organization, and Implementation

Mentoring plays a role in this program. For Oracle, mentoring is essential to ensuring the career progression of both men and women. The group is well advanced in this area, with mentoring programs (OWL: Oracle Women Leadership) available locally and by country. Its aim is to develop women and men in a very specific way by creating pairs of less experienced and more experienced colleagues. Mentoring, which enables the intuitive and tacit transfer of knowledge, puts the emphasis on feedback and the mentees' questions. It's part of Oracle's "self-driven learning." The program has around 70 percent female mentees and 30 percent male mentees.

A specific mentoring template has been developed to explain what mentees can expect and what mentors can contribute (experience, networking, team management and remote management, intercultural experience, etc.). A pilot mentoring group, composed of six women from different group subsidiaries (Oracle and companies acquired by the group) analyzed mentees' expectations and mentors' potential contributions. The mentoring pairs, of mixed genders generally, are carefully designed: two mentors are proposed to each mentee, who can speak with the proposed mentors and decide on one of them. Sometimes people who have not put themselves forward as mentors are requested, for example, to meet a specific requirement of the mentee.

Before starting, the program is presented to mentors and mentees along with the commitments and expectations required of each mentor and mentee. Meetings are organized regularly over breakfasts or lunches to encourage the sharing of experiences. Each mentor has a contact within the pilot management group to refer to if necessary. The group is responsible for all the experiences of the pairs. At the European level, discussions are also organized via a network that brings mentors together. And if the latter meet any problem in terms of listening, communicating, or restating, training is available to them.

Specific Roles

As advisors, the mentors support, encourage, and clarify matters for the mentees. Thanks to their experience, the mentors encourage the mentee to get involved in projects and to discuss the challenges constructively and objectively. This brings benefits also to the mentors: not only do they acquire new leadership skills, but they also gain personal and professional knowledge as well. Mentoring allows mentors to test out new ideas, improve networking, rediscover Oracle's organization, further develop their own networks, and use their coaching and advisory skills. Finally, the mentors' managerial skills also improve qualitatively. The mentoring program has a positive effect on the satisfaction and retention of colleagues.

Every beneficiary of the program must respect the aims agreed to at the start, and remain responsible for their achievement. The mentees acquire new skills and widen their knowledge base through discussions with the mentor. They must be open to their mentors' comments, and accept possible changes of direction. They must optimize the opportunities made available through mentoring, which is like a new kind of apprenticeship. Through the program, each mentee gains in confidence, benefits from encouragement and support, and becomes more visible in terms of career progression.

Toward an Intercompany Experience

An intercompany mentoring program is in place in subsidiaries in Rumania, the UK, Switzerland, and Spain. Open to both men and women, such programs attract a number of colleagues. The intercompany program decompartmentalizes the mentoring process and reduces the perceived confidentiality risk, which can make some people reluctant to consider internal company mentoring.

In Rumania, where the program was developed with GSK, Xerox, Renault, and Petrom, a survey of the mentors and the mentees measured the program's success: Was the mentor allowed to develop a network that opened doors? Was the mentee more networked than before? This intercompany mentoring allows participants not only to develop their networks, enhance their professional and individual profiles, but also opens up other industries, other ways of working, and other values.

12

VivaWomen! Program

Why has Publicis Groupe implemented a mentoring program?

We wanted to retain confidentiality in terms of performance (or nonperformance) of those participating in the program. The mentors and mentees therefore never come from the same subsidiary. This creates real confidentiality and generates trust. The VivaWomen! Program, open to women of the Groupe, has completed its pilot, and has been successful because it meets their expectations. Therefore anything that can support talented women—and men—to develop within the company and to achieve their ambitions, has to be encouraged.

What can we learn from this program, and what are the outcomes?

The first outcome is self-confidence, whatever mentoring program is followed. Confidence is a strong driver and to feel supported is an advantage. And this has repercussions in a range of work-related areas: greater confidence in internal relationships, a better understanding of teams and teamwork, more effective management systems aimed at the human elements and their relationships, and, of course, greater confidence in relationships with clients. There are also additional personal benefits, particularly in terms of personality and growth. In short, not only do we reap professional benefits, but also personal ones. And what's more, it's not only the mentee who benefits, but also the mentor.

What would you like to see happen after this experience?

It seems clear to me that we must continue this program. We've got to look a little closer at the extent to which the program has helped people to achieve their ambitions. The program is still in its infancy, and is being launched in different countries—taking into account the different local conditions and diverse cultures. It's based on sharing—simple, direct, easy, instant—the characteristics that the younger generation, who represent a large majority of our workforce, expect to see. We have to roll it out according to need. The VivaWomen! Program is based on a kind of generosity among its participants (women and men), a key value in my eyes, and certainly a factor of success.

AT PUBLICIS GROUPE, THE MAIN AIM OF MENTORING IS TO RETAIN TALENTED STAFF

The Mentoring Program at Publicis

Aims
Talent retention
Women's professional and personal development

Program Details and Aims
The VivaWomen! program includes mentoring, leadership, career navigation, and work-life balance, in order to increase

(continued)

(*continued*)

    the number of women leaders, improve women's career progression, improve work-life balances.

Outcomes

Increased motivation among employees and reduced sense of isolation; more concrete outcomes need to be assessed over time.

The VivaWomen! project aims to support women in their professional and personal development. The network is present in 16 towns (new countries were added at the end of 2013) and links together more than 2,000 women (irrespective of level in the group). The project's unique feature is that it is transversal, cutting across the group's subsidiaries and agencies.

Mentoring: A Priority for VivaWomen!?

Mentoring is one of the four major areas for VivaWomen!, the three others are Leadership, Career Navigation, and Work Life Balance.

Led by volunteers, each VivaWomen! network in the town or country decides its own agenda in line with local priorities. VivaWomen! launched a mentoring program in 2011, and this complements mentoring programs already running in some of the group's other subsidiaries or agencies.

The mentoring program's main feature is that it matches mentees (women only for two or three years now) and mentors (women and men with ten+ years of experience) from different subsidiaries, so as to create neutrality and equality in the mentoring relationship.

Mentoring is a priority for VivaWomen!, especially since a number of women reported they find it difficult to stay in some of the group's business sectors or within the communication industry in general. Since Publicis Groupe wishes to retain these talented women, it considers it essential that the women be heard, helped, and supported in their reflections and in their work.

Two Approaches to the Same Mentoring Program

Publicis Groupe's mentoring program is delivered in two ways.

One approach is through mentoring groups ("Mentoring Circles"). This is practiced in the United States because of the high numbers of mentees: groups of around 30-plus women are mentored in each session, which lasts half a day and is co-ordinated by a professional who explains each participant's role and responsibilities. During the session, the mentees are organized into small groups to discuss very precise topics with several mentors (men and women). The mentees benefit from the mentors' different experiences as well as from discussions with colleagues who have faced similar issues.

This very intensive approach benefits from the group dynamics, and each participant leaves feeling "nourished" by the discussions they have had with both mentors and with other mentees. Then it's up to the mentees to continue their paths. If necessary, relationships can be continued, but not necessarily as a group relationship.

The other approach is individual mentoring, face to face between mentoring pairs. This is practiced in several countries, including France, the UK, Spain, India, and others, and lasts over a period of six to nine months maximum. This approach, where the mentors are trained (and, in certain countries, the mentees too), facilitates more individualized mentoring over a longer period of time. The advantage of this approach lies in the mentoring relationship: thanks to the more regular discussions they have with their mentors, the mentees have more time to set goals, reflect, and implement them, and the mentors become allies with whom the mentees can tackle their projects and goals.

As this relationship lasts several months, the mentoring pair is matched very carefully by a small mentoring management team who monitor the pairs. In addition, the length of the relationship allows the mentees' reflections to mature and enables them to implement any decisions made.

Encouraging Results

These two approaches have specific and different advantages because of the time factor. But in both approaches, the mentees feel less isolated and have more confidence to go on. This is the fundamental aspect of the program: the mentees feel more motivated and stimulated in their work.

Around 150 women benefited from the program between 2011 and 2013. This number is fairly modest, but the feedback is very encouraging. More than 90 percent of participants said they were "very satisfied" with the program, and 100 percent recommended other employees to follow it because it was "useful" and "effective."

The tangible results (career progression, for example) are more complicated to measure because they do not happen over the short term or when the mentees are surveyed about the program. The issue for Publicis Groupe therefore is to measure more precisely what happens during mentoring and try to assess the program more concretely.

13

MixCity and Women's Leadership Initiative

INTERVIEW WITH MARIE-CLAIRE CAPOBIANCO, HEAD OF BNP PARIBAS FRENCH RETAIL BANKING

Why has BNP Paribas implemented a mentoring program?

Several parts of BNP Paribas have set up a mentoring program to offer tailored support to our high-potential employees. Each career step—recruitment, development, change of job—works toward building the group's culture and we invest a lot in these steps. Thus, for a long time now, we have run a "Management Academy" where our managers can study for their professional development. With the launch of a range of mentoring programs, we have undertaken another step in professional development, since we can now offer high added value to those employees selected to take part. In addition to the professional skills and expertise acquired through studies and through doing the job, mentoring adds knowledge and understanding of the whole professional landscape. It allows the mentees to hone their understanding of the role of job position vis-à-vis others or simply to build self-confidence and a desire to improve. This personal growth, which the mentees experience through their relationship with their mentors, can be a determining factor at a key moment in their careers. For women, who are still too few in the group's senior management, I strongly believe that mentoring is highly effective, because, much more than men, women need to learn to express the full range of their capabilities and their ambitions.

What can we learn from this program, and what are the outcomes?

I believe I can say that all the women in the group who have experienced the mentoring program are enthusiastic about it in terms of what they have learned. Each one has responded to the programs in a different way, because that's the great advantage of mentoring—it allows the mentee to discuss any subject, any issue, and inspires them to act. The mentees win, the mentors win, and the company wins.

What would you like to see happen after this experience?

It's clear that we want to continue this program! One point is of particular importance however, and that is the pairing of mentor and mentee. The quality of the contribution to the mentoring relationship is in putting the right mentor with the right mentee and ensuring the right psychological balance between them. This is the job of HR. Furthermore, to be really effective, mentoring must exist at the senior levels in the company, which limits the numbers of those who can take part. I've personally had the pleasure of mentoring two young and brilliant women who belong to different business lines and come from different countries. In each case, the relationship was rich, but also highly demanding on both sides. In devoting two hours a month to each of them over a period of a year, I was able to notice a change in the way they responded and reacted to specific situations. With hindsight, I can say that their development was worth the time I invested in them. To give time, to give attention, to learn of the responses and experiences of others—what better way than to share things that have actually happened? In conclusion, I am convinced that to offer our high-potential talents this opportunity to exchange ideas, in a structured way and off the record, is something that is worth doing. I'm convinced that it can help them find their right paths more quickly, and therefore help them to grow and to move into our key jobs.

BNP PARIBAS AS A PROACTIVE SUPPORTER OF WOMEN IN BUSINESS: A MENTORING PROGRAM

The Mentoring Program at BNP Paribas

Aims

Talent retention

Women's professional and personal development

Increase number of women in key posts of responsibility

Program Details and Aims

MixCity—internal network of women managers: to support women's career progression

Women in Leadership: to increase the number of women in leadership positions

Gender diversity: to fight discrimination and support diversity

Women's Leadership Initiative (sponsoring program): to promote women to posts of responsibility

Diversity Committee: to ensure diversity in recruitment and promotion

Outcomes

Twenty-two percent of senior management posts are held by women (target 25 percent)

Nine thousand employees trained in fighting discrimination and supporting diversity

Twenty-nine percent of women in the succession plan "Global High Potential"

(continued)

(continued)

Seven hundred members in MixCity network, as well as 3,200
women in 10 other such networks globally

More than 1000 women have followed professional and personal
development training

Catch-up plan for equal pay, began in 2008, has corrected 4,500+
pay differences

New quantifiable goals for women's promotion at every level of
management

Career progression from Women's Leadership Initiative (sponsoring program)

For several years, BNP Paribas has been proactive in supporting equality and diversity, particularly for women in the banking
group.

A Range of Measures

BNP Paribas' commitment to equality is evident in a range
of measures, which include the signing of the United Nations'
Women's Empowerment Principles in 2011, and the inclusion of
equal opportunity in the group's career development principles.

Other BNP Paribas actions include the following: at the end
of 2012, the signing of an agreement with the French Ministry of
Women's Rights to share its experience of equality at work; an
agreement to support its internal network of women managers,
BNP Paribas MixCity (reviewed and extended in 2013); and the
signing of the Parents' Charter at the end of 2008, and subsequent
joining of the related monitoring watchdog in 2009.

Furthermore, the bank proactively supports coaching and
mentoring in certain of its subsidiaries: Women in Leadership
(Property Division), support for gender diversity (Leasing Solutions Division), and Women's Leadership Initiative (Corporate
and Investment Banking Division), which is described later in
this chapter.

To complement actions already undertaken, the banking group
has also set up a Diversity Committee, and this monitors the

Human Resource Department's recruitment and career development strategies and implementation. The committee also ensures that the group's diversity strategy is operationalized within each subsidiary throughout the world.

In addition, the group has expanded its internal and external public relations strategy in order to ensure that the diversity message is communicated, has participated in governmental initiatives (surveys, enquiries, Diversity and Equality audits undertaken in Luxembourg and Canada, etc.) and organized Diversity Days in New York and Paris, and a Diversity Week in London.

Impressive Results

The range of measures has reaped rewards. The 2009 goal of achieving 20 percent of women in senior management by the end of 2012 was exceeded by one percentage point, and reached 22 percent in September 2014. By the end of 2014, the group achieved 25 percent. It targets 30 percent for 2020.

Support from the Chief Executives

Training and awareness campaigns to fight discrimination and promote diversity continue: 9,000 employees had been trained by the end of 2013, 3,500 of whom were in France.

In order to continue the trend, the group pays particular attention to the percentage of women in succession plans: at the end of 2012, there were 29 percent of women in the succession plan "Global High Potential."

The BNP Paribas MixCity network had 700 members at the end of 2013, a figure that is growing daily. In total, the group has 10 such networks around the world with 3,200 women who increasingly connect with each other. BNP Paribas MixCity offers professional and personal development sessions, which more than a thousand women have already followed. These sessions offer a range of topics: self-esteem, women and career positioning, life-work balance, and so on. A specific support program for women managers is also offered via individual and group coaching.

In 2013, three subsidiaries signed an agreement, or an additional clause to their existing agreement, on equality between men and women, making 16 agreements in total within the group in France. The fight to promote equal pay is manifested in a "catch-up" plan, which began in 2008, and, by 2010, almost 4,500 nonjustifiable pay differences had been corrected. Since then, the group has continued to correct any pay gaps and to prevent them occurring wherever possible.

For career development and promotions, new quantifiable goals for women's promotion at every level of the management hierarchy have been agreed upon. For example, in order to improve gender diversity for the key post of branch manager in the retail banking network, where women are still underrepresented, the group decided to increase the number of women in this post by six points between the beginning of 2013 and the end of 2015 (24 percent on December 31, 2012, to 30 percent on December 31, 2015).

Mentoring in Corporate and Institutional Banking

In 2012, Corporate and Institutional Banking (CIB), the investment banking division of BNP Paribas, launched a mentoring program named WLI (Women's Leadership Initiative). Its aim is to increase the presence of women in key posts throughout the bank. The pilot involved the mentoring of 28 of the bank's most talented women and was aimed at developing their careers in three ways:

1. Visibility: increasing women's visibility among the bank's directors in order to increase promotions
2. Opportunity: increasing the number of applications to posts of responsibility via mentoring
3. Ambition: developing awareness of stereotypes of women in terms of ambition

More than thirty of the most senior directors of CIB, including the chairman and chief executive, Alain Papiasse, became mentors in this program. Their involvement enabled the mentees to improve their positions in the bank, which facilitated career progression. The directors also provided leadership opportunities and opened their own networks in order to increase the mentees' visibility among other directors.

The pilot was rolled out in three phases.

Phase 1: the mentees each participated in a 360° leadership analysis and then met together in order to understand their roles and responsibilities in the program.

Phase 2: the mentor/mentee pairs met to agree on the terms of their contract and their method of working together, and to identify career progression opportunities.

Phase 3: the mentors and mentees took part in a workshop aimed at getting the best possible performances out of the women as leaders. This seminar aimed to develop awareness of how men and women manage, and a review of the methods by which women managers can give the best of themselves.

This program aims to see at least 25 percent of mentees benefit from career development over a period of three years by developing their leadership skills. In addition, it encourages the mentors to offer specific opportunities for career development to the women. More generally, the program will enable the bank to improve the mentors' and mentees' knowledge and to encourage the creation of actions aimed at promoting women. The Women's Initiatives Network, or WIN, has absolutely increased their confidence, enhanced their profiles, and frankly, improved their managers' understanding of their roles and potential. And then the network that they have developed means they're more likely to know whether there's a job opening in this spot or that spot. They're more likely to be able to call a woman who's in a group or in a job posting and connect with them in a self-help way. And then, of course, we have a mentoring program that's actually a year-long investment in their professional development.

14

Women's Initiative Network and Reverse Mentoring Program

INTERVIEW WITH KAREN PEETZ, PRESIDENT OF BNY MELLON

Women have to have the confidence to be heard and to lead.

Karen was promoted to president of BNY Mellon in 2013. She has worked in banking for 30 years and was the company's first female vice chair. Karen is passionate about fostering a responsible, risk-sensitive banking culture and making the business case for diverse talent. She is also a leading player in the finance sector's changing risk and regulation frameworks, aimed at strengthening reliability and rebuilding trust in the sector.

Since 2009, BNY Mellon has witnessed a 100 percent increase in the number of women and a 35 percent increase in the number of people from diverse racial and ethnic backgrounds at

Executive Committee, Operating Committee, and Regional Operating Committee levels. Forty-four percent of the global workforce are women; 36 percent of the VPs are women; 26 percent of the MDs are women; and 19 percent of the Executive Committee are women.

Women in the Economy

How do you see the role of women in today's economic world?

I think that the good news is that companies around the world are recognizing that with women being at least half of the world's population, it's very important that they get engaged, if nothing else, in order to optimize economic opportunities. And when you look at it that way, you realize that the country that does the best job of mobilizing women will end up performing better.

> The country that does the best job of mobilizing women will end up performing better.

I think we are moving from what was an altruistic suggestion to a much more economic imperative. And that's very healthy and will, I think, create much more opportunity as countries in various ages and stages of development understand that. And with efforts like the push for board membership, and efforts to promote women and have parity—that's kind of the icing on the cake.

Do you think women managers bring any particular advantages to the company? If so, what?

Yes, I do think that many of the typical female skills—like being highly collaborative, having strong intuition about people, understanding risk, and solid organizational skills—tend to be high on the list. Certainly anybody who can run a career and run a family has to be pretty organized. And the female approach can be hugely helpful to traditionally male bastions such as business. The flip side, though, is that the women have to have the confidence to be heard and to lead; so it's great if you have that skill set, but if you cannot get yourself into a position to be heard or to lead, then it doesn't matter if you have all those softer skills.

> Certainly anybody who can run a career and run a family has to be pretty organized. And the female approach can be hugely helpful to traditionally male bastions such as business.

Do you think, given the bad press that the banking sector has had over the last few years, that the presence of more women at the top will have a positive effect on that sector?

Yes, I think that we can't say, "Women would have done this or that differently," because who knows what more senior women would have done. But I think that the same skill set that I just talked about—the ability to collaborate and to come to mutual agreements about solutions and really get people involved—is the new expectation, particularly for the younger generation. And I think that the changing appetite from an autocratic to a more democratic, from a top down to a more participative, leadership style will play to women's strengths as well.

Obstacles Facing Women

What are the major obstacles that prevent women from attaining key decision-making posts?

McKinsey has done some excellent research, and they've come up with what are statistically significant either derailers or inhibitors for women. And I happen to agree with them.

The Number 1 obstacle is "lack of sponsors": sponsor being someone who is in the room with the power to actually do something for you—and certainly in my own career, that's been instrumental: I wouldn't have progressed to where I am without strong, and frankly all male, sponsors. That's the first inhibitor.

> The Number 1 obstacle is "lack of sponsors": sponsor being someone who is in the room with the power to actually do something for you.

The second obstacle is "lack of role models." That, of course, becomes a self-fulfilling prophecy: if you don't see senior women then you don't believe that you can actually do it. That's changing as we get more CEOs and women in senior places—women such as the Angela Merkels, the very senior female politicians, and Hillary Clinton, for instance.

> The second obstacle is "lack of role models."

The other inhibitors, which I think are hugely impactful, are two categories of prejudice—and of course nobody really likes to talk about that. The first one is prejudice about women and preconceived notions about what they can do or want to do—stereotypes, if you will.

And the second factor is prejudice about ourselves—that's the limiting thoughts or limiting horizons that many women have, whether it's through socialization or self-doubt. They have prejudices about themselves and so when others have prejudices about them, then women feel there's nothing wrong with that.

Overcoming the Obstacles

At BNY Mellon, 44 percent of your global workforce are women, 36 percent of your VPs are women, 26 percent of your MDs are women, and 19 percent of your Executive Committee are woman. So BNY Mellon has made great steps forward in the promotion of women.

How can we support women to overcome these obstacles?

I think we have to help women with their mind-sets—that concept of prejudice about ourselves. You need to have the right mind-set to succeed. And what's interesting here in the United States is that they're correlating long-term success career-wise with athletic participation as a young girl. That actually happened to me: I was heavily involved in competitive athletics, and they're saying—and I agree—that learning about competition, self-reliance within a team, winning, but also losing, is hugely helpful to get into that mind-set. In many ways, it's a marathon, not a sprint, and you're going to have ups and downs. You're going to win some and lose some. And as you go up the chain, you're judged on how you handle both—the losing and the winning—and how you stick with it. Now that I've been thirty-plus years in banking, I can think of whole years that weren't that fun. But when I look back on it, I learned something; I grew; I developed; and I stuck with it.

> You need to have the right mind-set to succeed.

The other thing to help women succeed is encouraging them to get diverse work experience. Many women get stuck in historically female-type roles—and they may get to the top of whatever pyramid that is, such as legal or HR, where females have historically done well. But it's more unusual to see women in business roles. So you must not get complacent at an early stage if you have a long-term desire to get to the top; you have to be constantly developing and expanding.

So those are broad principles, but what we do at BNY Mellon to support women is that we have some structures that we call "Employee Resource Groups." They're not only for women—they're also for people of color, people from diverse backgrounds, and people with disabilities. They are networks where people can gain exposure, professional development, and business experience in a low-threat environment.

> Many women get stuck in historically female type roles.... But it's more unusual to see women in business roles.

We also have begun something that we call a "Nine Box Talent Review," which we're integrating into our organization. It's a way of calibrating talent within every group in the company. What I think is great about it is that everyone's name has to be on the piece of paper. Therefore, it captures diverse people in a very clear and transparent way of talking about talent. Everybody's name has to be on the paper, so people that might not have been considered otherwise will have both their performance and potential discussed and calibrated. It's part and parcel of the appraisal system. Management teams are being tasked to not only put names on paper, but to discuss how to develop those people—and then that smaller group of top talent gets special development and attention.

Do you think that your Employee Resource Group WIN has been specifically successful in promoting women in BNY Mellon?

The leadership experiences that many women have availed themselves of within our Women's Initiatives Network, or WIN, have absolutely increased their confidence, and enhanced their profile. And the network that they have developed means they're more likely to know whether there's a job opening in this spot or that spot.

I don't think we can point to *We did this and then we got that*. But the leadership experiences that many women have availed themselves of within our Women's Initiatives Network, or WIN, have absolutely increased their confidence, enhanced their profile, and frankly, improved their managers' understanding of their roles and potential. And then the network that they have developed means they're more likely to know whether there's a job opening in this spot or that spot. They're more likely to be able to call a woman who's in a group or in a job posting and connect with them in a self-help way. And then, of course, we have a mentoring program that's actually a year-long investment in their professional development.

What is the Reverse Mentoring Program?

I have a very high-potential mentor in our Markets Group; and at my first meeting with her, she said, "So, where are your goals, and what are you actually doing?" You know, I was a little intimidated so I showed her not only the goals that had been submitted to the board, that I was on the hook for, but I also showed her the summary of my performance for the year, to really give her a sense of the level I was operating at, the kind of goals, and the formality that she might not have been as aware of. But it was just a funny conversation—I was explaining myself to this twenty-two-year-old—which I do at home all the time. And, growing out of this generation-type initiative, we have a new Employee Resource Group, or an Affinity Group, called GenEdge, which is meant for that generation to engage them in a similar way, with those from other generations, as we've done with women and people of color, and so on. So it's good.

So what was the goal of the Reverse Mentoring Program?

It was a way of taking some high-potential junior people and connecting them to senior people for their experience, wisdom, and hopefully motivation. But equally it was to connect the more senior people to younger people who have been recruited for their potential, but who are pretty far down in the organization. And to get their views (and I have to say my mentor is incredibly mature) of the kind of things senior management should be thinking about to relate to their generation.

The Mentoring Program at BNY Mellon Bank

Aims

Talent retention: Integrate women returning from long-term leave; support career progression

Connectivity and networking

Collaboration and knowledge sharing

Bottom-line performance

Program Details and Aims

Women's Initiative Network: to increase the number of women in senior positions

Re-entry program for women who have taken long-term leave: to improve retention

Mentoring program: to improve career progression and knowledge of the group

Reverse mentoring program: to provide senior executives with knowledge of what younger colleagues expect of the group

Outcomes

One hundred percent increase in the number of women in the workforce (now 44 percent of the global workforce)

Thirty-six percent of vice presidents are women.

Twenty-six percent of managing directors are women; 19 percent of the Executive Committee are women.

INTERVIEW WITH JEAN WYNN, MANAGING DIRECTOR AND CHIEF ADMINISTRATIVE OFFICER OF BNY MELLON'S OFFICE OF THE PRESIDENT

Jean Wynn provides oversight for BNY Mellon's company-wide initiatives in the areas of organizational development, sales effectiveness, and employee engagement. She also leads BNY Mellon's Global Innovation Program. Jean is co-chair of BNY Mellon's Women's Initiative Network (WIN) and is co-founder of the Wall Street Women's Alliance. For its success in promoting the advancement of women in the company, the leaders of BNY Mellon's WIN were named a Top Team (2009) by *American Banker Magazine/US Banker*, as part of the annual review of the most powerful women on Wall Street.

Since 2009, BNY Mellon has witnessed a 100 percent increase in the number of women and a 35 percent increase in the number of people from diverse racial and ethnic backgrounds at Executive Committee, Operating Committee, and Regional Operating Committee levels: 44 percent of the global workforce are women; 36 percent of the VPs are women; 26 percent of the MDs are women; and 19 percent of the Executive Committee are women.

How do you see the role of women in today's economic/financial world?

There is ... a widely recognized growing economic paradigm shift where women are becoming much more financially pronounced. There are more women who have expanded their wealth due to ... being in the workforce for an extended period of time and at higher levels.

Certainly all the statistics point to the fact that women are commanding a growing share of financial assets in economies around the world, and they control a considerable amount of spending, roughly two-thirds in the United States as an example. This is finally being more widely recognized as a growing economic

paradigm shift where women are becoming much more financially pronounced. There are more women who have expanded
their wealth due to more of them being in the workforce for an
extended period of time and at higher levels, albeit we have not
seen as many as we would like rise to the top ranks. Nonetheless,
there has been progress and, as a result, we see more financial
independence on the part of women. So to that end, businesses
should begin to re-orient themselves to this demographic shift, in
recognition of that command of that purse, and start looking at
their business model and go-to-market strategies on the consumer
side as well as on the institutional side.

Do you think women managers bring any particular advantages to the company? If so, what?

If the clients making the decisions are women, then you need to
reflect that in your company as well in terms of having women
in your company who can match off against that and mirror that
client base. Companies can benefit from management style and
traits women are known for, namely listen, consult, ask questions
versus talk, give orders, and answer questions. In general, the leadership style of women tends to be more collaborative, which is a
style welcomed in companies today.

> Women can provide a different perspective on the thinking
> process.

There are always exceptions, but women can provide a different
perspective on the thinking process, and, as innovation becomes
more and more important in companies, doing things differently,
leading change, and drawing upon more diverse thought processes,
all point to advantages women can bring. Plus all the stats confirm
the business case: put more women in senior management and on
boards, and the company performs better, full stop.

> Put more women in senior management and on boards, and
> the company performs better, full stop.

What are the major obstacles that prevent women from attaining key decision-making posts?

I think there's still an element of unconscious bias. This stems from society and upbringing, and it's more pervasive in certain cultures across the globe than others. So as an example, this can lead to men making decisions around who is right for a position or who might be tapped for that assignment, and they are not necessarily doing it consciously. And then there is the fundamental biological obstacle, the fact that women do need to take time off to have a family. And as a result of that, there continues to be a certain stigma putting women at a disadvantage. As a result, they may opt out themselves, and that's another problem in terms of their confidence and ability to take action with the mind-set and resilience to make it work.

What advice or support can we give to women to overcome these obstacles? What do you do at BNY Mellon to support women to advance in the organization?

> Organizations need to concentrate on this a bit more: staying connected with women who go out on leave, making them feel connected, and giving them that support and encouragement, so they want to come back.

As much as we try to support women, I do think organizations need to concentrate on this a bit more: staying connected with women who go out on leave, making them feel connected, and giving them that support and encouragement, so they want to come back when they feel it appropriate, and feel confident in doing so. But, if they do want to take more extended leave, then I think there are some successful programs, and we as a company are going to be giving it a try with our WIN group. This involves establishing a re-entry program for women who have opted out for a period to come back and to get reacquainted with the workplace and by doing project work, that is, short-term assignments that will enable us and them to decide whether this test drive really works. Do they want to come back and under what circumstances, and at the same time, they are accomplishing some work for us by getting some projects done, and this also gives them something on their resume even if they don't get placed permanently with our company. So we're in the process of investigating that now, and we do think that that's an important thing to have out there to convince women that we are committed to that process and that we do want to retain the talent that they represent.

Can you tell me a little more about WIN?

WIN is our Women's Initiatives Network, and we're about eleven years into this now. It was our first employee resource group in the company, and it was championed by Karen Peetz. She got the idea right after attending a Women's Bond Club event in New York City. She looked around the room and saw that there were many impressive senior women throughout the industry represented at this dinner. She learned what many were doing in terms of the mentoring and support for women, and thought that should be replicated within our company. So we joined that organization and there were a few of us that got together and said, "What can we do to help other women in our company?" That was kind of the formation of our WIN group eleven years ago. And since that time, we've filled some gaps that the company had with respect to some developmental needs. We also networked and connected through community service. We got involved in the American Cancer Society's breast cancer walk, and the Heart Association's Go Red for Women campaign.

From there, we put more structure around it, got a budget, put in more governance, and devised a mentoring program as well, which was the first formal mentoring program in the company at that time. And then from there, that was the launch pad and since then, we've just expanded across the globe; we started really in New York and London first, and now we have 56 chapters worldwide and over 5,000 members, and we're still going strong.

Our mentoring program was set up very early on, so we were the pioneer in the company to start that. The largest benefit from the mentoring program is about providing connectivity across the company—we are a very large company—so part of what our WIN organization has been able to help the company do is certainly to drive more collaboration and knowledge about the company itself, so that people just know more about what we do and how a network within the company can help them in their day-to-day jobs.

The other thing WIN just launched, and this is in a pilot stage, is a Reverse Mentoring program, which takes our millennial WIN members and puts them with mentees on our Executive Committee, including our CEO, CFO, and president—so Karen Peetz is being mentored by a millennial. It's in its pilot stages but again, I think it does draw on more connectivity between the generations and allows for some of our senior executives to see how things are resonating throughout the company at the more junior levels.

And then the fundamental goal for our women's group is really to drive bottom line impact for the company—strategically we try to gear all of our activities, and get all of our membership, aware of this goal. WIN is very good for women to get involved in, because of the visibility and the career opportunities it creates. Ultimately, what we really are trying to do is create that bottom line impact for the company so that we're looked upon, truly, as a business resource group. And we have been able to successfully do that by connecting, and sharing our learning, with our clients, who are, in many cases, in the financial industry itself. We were a pioneer in forming the Wall Street Women's Alliance (WSWA), which is a very informal group, a "network of networks" of women's group leaders who get together to share what's working and what's not, and collectively try to solve the problems, so that we're all improving our networks. Hopefully, by pulling more women up the ranks, and therefore the industry, we'll make a difference to our industry collectively.

I'll just also say that our women's group is not only for women—we have a concerted effort to draw men into leadership roles within the governance structure of our WIN organization—deliberately—we think that's really important. Our Executive Sponsor is a man on the Executive Committee, so very senior, and he has been a terrific advocate and supporter for what we are doing.

Part IV

MENTORING PROGRAM SUCCESS STORIES

MENTORING AND SPONSORING PRODUCE A RANGE of benefits—not only for the mentee, but also for the mentor. In this section, mentees and mentors tell us about how they've benefited from their mentoring programs.

These benefits include changes in their attitudes about work, in their personalities and in their ambitions, positive impacts on their careers, and improved relationships with their colleagues. Tabitha Coombe tells how mentoring made her more aware of career opportunities within BNP Paribas, and raised her ambitions. A fellow mentor, but in ENGIE, Matthias Curnier describes mentoring as win-win, saying that it's a great opportunity to meet new people and understand new ways of thinking. Matthias's mentee, Paola Vezzaro, as an Italian in a French group, said she wanted mentoring to educate her about how the group worked, and what was sacred and taboo—and she got what she was looking for and more: mentoring helped her career progression, and, now that she is geographically far from the group's head office, mentoring enables her to stay in touch with the heart of decision-making and strategy.

Paula Craythorne, at Oracle, views mentoring as sponsoring—as a relationship that can tangibly help her to develop her career, and her colleague, Nicoleta Apostol, says that mentoring works if you have a clear understanding of what it can do for you: have a tangible goal, be ready to take the initiative, and aim to become visible. Nicoleta says that mentoring gave her the strategic insights that she felt she needed in order to progress. For her mentor, Giovanna Sangiorgi, mentoring was initially about giving back, helping and challenging women to be comfortable with leadership and power—but after some years, it helped her to know herself better, to know what she was good at, and what made her a good leader.

At Publicis, both mentee Charlotte Guillabert, and mentor Michele Gilbert, reflect upon the benefits their relationship brings. For Charlotte, it is about career development and how to attain a senior position; whereas Michele believes that mentoring can help employees find a route through difficult situations, since the sharing of experiences and talking to someone who can see the bigger picture can help to relieve any anxiety and stress you might feel when you begin to have doubts about your abilities.

For Regina Meredith-Carpeni, at BNY Mellon, including men in the mentoring relationship can give women the exposure and recognition that helps them to be considered for the next promotion or assignment—she feels this is particularly important for women caught in what she refers to as the "frozen middle," those women who have fallen off the radar of "top talent" once they've taken a leave of absence for child-raising. In addition to a traditional mentoring program, BNY Mellon also runs reverse mentoring, where senior executives are mentored by junior millenials. For mentor Yoon Park, recently arrived in the bank, mentoring gives her an understanding of the company's strategic initiatives and projects. For her mentee, Jeff Kuhn, talking to Yoon gives him the opportunity to understand what motivates the millenials in the bank and what they're looking for, and how he can apply that knowledge to developing the talent in the bank.

Part IV of the book tells us exactly what it's like to be involved in a mentoring program, both as a mentee and as a mentor.

15

BNP Paribas Corporate & Institutional Banking (CIB)

INTERVIEW WITH TABITHA COOMBE (MENTEE)

Mentoring made me look at my career in a different way.

Tabitha is in charge of the structured financing legal team within the Corporate & Institutional Banking (CIB) of BNP Paribas.

How long have you worked in France?

After three years as an associate at Slaughter and May, a London-based UK law firm, I joined the Paris branch in 1999 and stayed for six years. Then, in 2005, I joined BNP Paribas as a lawyer in the team responsible for international financing of energy and raw materials and project financing. In 2009, I was appointed as deputy director of the team, and in 2013 I was appointed director. In the meantime, the team had expanded into aircraft and ship financing, and had grown from 7 to 16 lawyers.

Before joining the WLI (Women's Leadership Initiative) program, had you previously been mentored?

Not formally, no. In the law firm, you usually work for a few associates, and mentoring can take place in an informal way. When I learnt that I'd been chosen to take part in the WLI pilot, I was delighted. I hoped that the program would help me to understand the group better. When I started at BNP Paribas, I spent a lot of time working on files, and I got to know only my in-house clients. However, BNP Paribas is a major group, and although I knew a lot of people, my network was limited to the activity in which I worked. I knew that I had to extend the network in order to understand how the group worked.

How was the program for you?

> By the time we got to the end of the mentoring program, we realized that our mentors often encountered the same problems as us.

I was in a group of four women mentored by two directors: François Freyeisen and a man in charge of capital markets. It was an excellent combination. To share the mentoring experience with three other women was very interesting since we were able to share our worries and experiences. Our discussions were good for both the mentors and the mentees. Indeed, by the time we got to the end of the mentoring program, we realized that our mentors often encountered the same problems as us. At the beginning, everyone spent an entire day together, then, over the nine months of the program, we had three online meetings during which we discussed different subjects. Our mentors also arranged meetings for us with senior women executives within BNP Paribas, and we were encouraged to attend their steering committees. Thanks to WLI, my understanding of the group, outside of the CIB, has grown substantially. The program ended with another full day with all the participants. As our group found the experience a little too short, we decided to continue our discussions over lunch meetings.

What did you think at the end of the program?

> The mentoring program benefited me in several ways: it made me aware of the career opportunities for women ... mentoring demonstrated that women can legitimately expect to have careers that lead to positions of responsibility, and that the bank's future is also the future of its women.... Mentoring enabled me to have a more transversal view of the various career paths, and it gave me a network.... Mentoring made me look at my career in a different way.

There's a difference in the proportion of women in the various divisions and the proportion in positions of responsibility. This program is one of the bank's ways of changing the situation. The mentoring program benefited me in several ways: it made me aware of the career opportunities for women aiming to hold positions of responsibility—mentoring demonstrated that women can legitimately expect to have careers that lead to positions of responsibility, and that the bank's future is also the future of its women. In addition, mentoring enabled me to have a more transversal view of the various career paths, and it gave me a network, which I can go to when I want a different view of my own career path—not to mention the network of other mentees and my mentors. Mentoring made me look at my career in a different way. The steering committees of tomorrow will reflect the balance of men and women that currently exists in the teams of today. The WLI program is aimed at preparing the group for these changes by creating a meeting place for directors and women who have the ambition to construct a professional career.

INTERVIEW WITH FRANÇOIS FREYEISEN (MENTOR)

> All my mentees developed and have been promoted.

François is in charge of compliance within Corporate & Institutional Banking (CIB), a division of BNP Paribas.

In 2012, CIB launched a pilot mentoring program. Why did you take part?

I've worked at BNP Paribas since 1979. Until the beginning of the 1990s, I was a banker, then management controller. After that, I worked in the markets in Paris, London, and Tokyo, before coming back to Paris in 2010 to take up my current post. When I heard about the WLI program, I said yes immediately. Over a period of several months, I mentored four women whom I already knew professionally, and I was therefore very interested in getting to know them personally. A few months before the start of the program, I had organized an informal mentoring between a young woman from Brussels and a female colleague from Paris who had a brilliant career within the bank. Personally, I've never had an official mentor, but throughout my career, I've benefited from informal mentoring by people I've respected and with whom I've stayed in touch ever since—even after their departure or retirement from the bank. Mentoring is a question of affinity.

Did you prepare for this role before starting out?

We attended a workshop for mentors where one of us explained what was expected. We were given a sort of route map. The French mentees seemed a bit surprised by the program, perhaps for cultural reasons. They wondered why they needed support. Perhaps it was a question of pride or skepticism, as they wanted to believe that a person, man or woman, should be rewarded on merit. There was certainly this sort of tendency in my group, where two of the mentees were a bit wary of the approach. They saw it as a sort of condescension, afraid they'd be seen as lagging behind, as if they were recipients of charity or that they deserved pity. However, this had no impact at all on the mentoring relationship!

How did the mentoring go?

My group consisted of an Irish woman based in Ireland, a French woman whose origin was Cambodian, a Belgian-Canadian living in France, and an English woman who had lived in France for some time, Tabitha Coombe. There were three ways we could work together: meetings and individual lunches to get to know each other better; three sessions with all the groups—at the beginning, halfway through and at the end; and online meetings with experts. One day an American woman talked about how to succeed in a man's world, giving advice about how to dress and hairstyles, which led to enormous hilarity among the French! There we had another cultural difference! In the mentoring context, I invited my mentees to attend, individually, an executive committee meeting to see how it worked. They discovered the type of topics that were discussed, participated in discussions, and, more specifically, learnt how, when we don't agree, to compromise and reach a workable consensus.

Let's speak about Tabitha Coombe …

> I was able to talk to Tabitha about my experience and explain to her how to alternate between operational posts and specialist posts, or to move geographically. The interest is to vary the posts, and not to remain in one post forever.

Tabitha wanted to understand the internal politics of the bank. She's a remarkable lawyer who has had her head in files for a long time, reading contracts, recommending solutions. This type of work is very technical. She was already deputy director of her team and was wondering how she, as a specialist, could move on in the organization, and how to combine that with management.

The more political aspects of how the bank worked interested her. Like the other three women in my group, she wanted to know how to use her skills to progress and find a way through a path that seemed full of traps. As I was also a specialist, I was able to talk to Tabitha about my experience and explain to her how to alternate between operational posts and specialist posts, or to move geographically. The interest is to vary the posts, and not to remain in one post forever. It's also important to cultivate a multicultural view. Since the end of the program, with no cause-and-effect relationship, Tabitha has been promoted and now has full responsibility for her team!

What has this experience brought you?

As a man, and moreover as a French man, I was a little skeptical about the program, thinking that I'd look like the kind of man who lectures weak women, some of whom were actually more qualified than me! It was a mistake. I got to know them personally, and even though the program is over, I always get their news, and we have lunch together every six months or so. My four mentees have all received promotions or progressed in their careers! I don't pretend to think it's anything to do with the mentoring program, but I'd say it's just a happy coincidence!

INTERVIEW WITH MARGUERITE BURGHARDT (MENTEE)

My mentor has been a wonderful guide.

Marguerite directs "Strategy & Products" a team based in different locations in Europe which aims at providing Global services to the Transaction Banking Hubs in CIB (excluding Cash Management), and to the Trade P&L owners in the Retail Poles FRB (French Retail Banking), Fortis, BnL (Banca Nazionale del Lavoro), and IRB (International Retail Banking).

You joined BNP Paribas in 1993. What has your career path been like?

I have been working as a CIB Coverage Banker for six years (three years in Paris, three years in Madrid-Spain). After that, back in France, I joined the newly created "Group Risk Management" where I acted as a delegation holder with a Senior Credit Officer role, in charge of Structured Finance (Media & Telecom Finance, LBO, Project Finance, Corporate Acquisition Finance). I then joined Fixed Income as Head of Counterparty Risk, covering all counterparty risk issues globally, both at Corporates and at Financial Institutions. Following these very exciting six years at Global Markets, I joined Transaction Banking two years ago. Each time I changed positions it has been a huge challenge, with high technical and networking barriers. Difficult challenges are a real fuel for me.

You were chosen to take part in the WLI mentoring pilot. How was it for you?

My mentor, Constance Chalchat, immediately invested time and commitment to make me understand that more progress, more visibility was achievable and that I had to increase self-confidence. She invited me to attend the GECD (Global Equities and Commodity Derivatives) EXCO (Executive Committee) in order to make me understand that EXCO membership is not "out of reach."

> From the mentoring, I learned something that is essential for career progression: how to market yourself internally.

This investment of her time gave me a lot of pleasure. We also stayed in touch by telephone. Throughout the program, and even today, she works hard to make herself available.

Has the mentoring had a good influence on your career?

My career development isn't directly linked to the mentoring but is more a result of years of work. It's not because I've got a mentor that I get a promotion! But I learned something that is essential for career progression: how to market yourself internally—as a leader, for example, or whatever it is you want to be noticed for. As in all companies, though BNP Paribas is especially big, there's a tendency to spend your days in the little teams, and it can be quite difficult for people to move out of these comfort zones. This is where Constance's mentoring has been fantastic. She talked to me about certain people who I had to meet, people who worked in departments quite far removed from mine. This link with Constance opened doors and enabled me to meet a wider group of people. She played the role of intermediary to begin with to ensure I was in touch with such-and-such a person, then I took over.

> Constance opened doors and enabled me to meet a wider group of people. She played the role of intermediary to begin with to ensure I was in touch with such-and-such a person, then I took over.

I can never thank her enough for insisting on self-confidence and the importance of self promotion: thanks to her input, I joined an EXCO when I last changed positions two years ago. It has become a reality!

To sum up, can we say that if mentoring creates some opportunities, it can also offer you something precious?

Indeed, yes. The increased self-confidence, and the mentoring, have turned me into a more committed employee of BNP Paribas, one who buys into the bank's success.

What could women do to be better represented in the senior ranks of the hierarchy?

The banking sector is especially dominated by men; few women are in positions of responsibility. It's interesting to see how such women are viewed and how they find their balance. When you want to be respected, you can't appear too aggressive; otherwise, you're not well regarded. I always ask women in powerful positions how they managed to break through the barriers. My younger colleagues, whom I try to mentor in an informal way, ask me the same questions. Sometimes, I tell myself that women have to work a lot harder than men in order to be respected. Statistics show that men apply for positions even if they don't feel ready, whereas women reflect and defer what they want, arguing that they'll be ready for this promotion next year. But for me, a woman must raise her hand and go for it. I tell my current deputy, who is a young woman: if you don't ask, you don't get. When my female colleagues hesitate to take responsibility, I tell them that it shows a lack of self-confidence:

> Think about what you want and go for it, but show that you've got a strategy and that this is what you want—in this way you'll inspire confidence in whomever you're talking to.

I am fortunate to have four sons at home, so I won't have to teach them how to promote their female specificity!! I will rather let them know that the world has changed and that they will have to compete against women at par with men, in their professional lives.

INTERVIEW WITH CONSTANCE CHALCHAT (MENTOR)

Men need to face up to the problem of women in order to change.

Constance is in charge of People Development, marketing, public relations, and innovation in the Global Equities and Commodity Derivatives department of BNP Paribas CIB.

What is your main motivation at work?

Effectiveness. And to do that, we have to move the boundaries! I have always been driven by that. And so, after finishing my commercial school, I went to the United States because I wanted to see the country and learn other methods than those I'd been taught at school: I worked in strategic marketing at Danone in New York for three months.

On my return to Europe, as I wanted to get to know a more innovative area, I joined Nike, always in strategic marketing, and stayed there for three years. I then went to a consultancy company for three years followed by a year in the Internet bubble. I then searched for a place to apply my skills in strategy and marketing—somewhere where everything needed doing. In my view, that was in insurance and finance. Chance played a hand in things, and I was headhunted by BNP Paribas. I joined the markets division in 2001 in order to develop a marketing plan for derivatives on shares; then my responsibilities changed as things developed. Among other things, I took over public relations, then events management, created client services, applied lean management to the front office, and dealt with the problem of costs, of innovation. I'm currently in charge of seven or eight areas and am on the executive committee of our subsidiary. Wherever we can add value, that's what I'm interested in!

Why did you agree to take part in the WLI mentoring program?

During my career, I've been lucky enough to have bosses who trusted me. For example, my current boss listens to me and gives me advice, but we still have differences of opinion. It seems difficult to me to have one's own boss as a mentor. Moreover, too few women hold positions of responsibility in the bank, but as one of them, I would have liked to benefit from advice and the experience of a woman some years ago. It's why I want to support young women and help them to progress along the right path. When I was asked to become a mentor for WLI, I didn't hesitate for a second. As I'd co-written the book *Mission Possible—The Women's Way* to help women progress in the company, the Human Resource Department naturally turned to me. For me, diversity is very important, since it concerns women, multiculturalism, and the rights of parents.

You mentored a group of four young women working in a division connected to yours. How was that?

My group consisted of a French woman, an English, an Australian, and an American. At the same time, I was also mentoring a young French woman in my own activity, under a connected mentoring program. I saw each of them monthly, at least for half an hour, usually three-quarters of an hour, but the first meeting lasted 60 minutes. In the beginning, I listened to them to see how I could help. And if I had an interesting experience to share with them, I did so. For example, I told them about the time when a very senior executive in my group met each member of the executive committee, but I was the last person he had to see, and he only had five minutes left because all my colleagues—men, by the way—had eaten up his time. I was a little fed up of this, so I took the allotted half an hour and told him that I was counting on him to give me as much time as my colleagues. I offered to arrange meetings for my mentees with people from other business areas for them to gain visibility. For Marguerite, my French mentee, I got her to participate in one of my division executive committee meetings. One of the topics addressed was quite close to Marguerite's area of responsibility, and she stepped up and gave all executive committee members really interesting insights and pieces of advice. She got everyone very interested and gained significant visibility through this participation. With my American mentee, I spoke to her about events that I had organized in Paris to promote women. In launching something similar in New York, my American mentee really gained visibility at very senior levels.

Would you like to continue mentoring?

Even though the WLI pilot is finished, I continue to follow and meet up with my mentees. I'd be happy to continue with other people, and I'm happy to be a role model for certain women. But I'd like to give priority to male mentors because they need to understand the problems faced by women if they are to bring about changes. I'm the only woman on the executive committee, and I spoke about the program with my colleagues. Mentoring has to be win-win. Women have a lot of psychological blocks that stop them getting on. In my opinion, if a man tells them it's all in their heads, it will have more impact than if it were me telling them. Women need to hear it from a man, and that opens men's eyes as well! What counts is the added value, not the time spent in the office! This female block is interesting … mentoring seems to me to be important therefore, but the real subject is the structure: women have to decide to listen to themselves and to make their own way through their careers by bringing added value and by increasing their own value. This means a huge psychological step. A mentor cannot bring all of that—but it is a very useful tool, though it's not the only one.

16

ENGIE

INTERVIEW WITH MATHIAS CURNIER (MENTOR)

Believe in yourself! I am always surprised by women's lack of confidence in themselves. **Dare!** Women should dare to ask for promotion even if they feel that the job is not for them! **Trust!** I believe that women's positions will improve because men will understand that it is important for everyone within the organization.

Mathias joined ENGIE in 1996, and is currently Deputy Executive Vice-President, Communications & Marketing, Environmental & Social Responsibility. He has worked with two mentees in the ENGIE Mentoring Program and recently mentored Paola Vezzaro.

Can you tell me briefly about your business career?

I joined the ENGIE group in 1996. From 1996 till 2001, I was successively Market Analyst and Business Development Manager for United Water and Degremont, subsidiaries of SUEZ Environment in the United States. Back in France in 2002,

I became Marketing Programme Manager in the areas of pulp and paper, oil and pharmaceutical industries for SUEZ Industrial Solutions. I am now Deputy to the Executive Vice President of ENGIE, Communications, Marketing, Environmental & Social Responsibility.

I hold a bachelor of business administration and an MBA in marketing and strategy from the Fox School of Business, Temple University, Philadelphia, in the United States. I've been a member of the board of Culturespaces and Culturespaces Foundation since 2010. I am a member of the French American Foundation.

Do you feel there are any obstacles to women achieving key posts of responsibility within companies?

It is clear to me that women's career paths within companies can be more difficult than those of their male counterparts. It is not a question of qualifications, willingness, or a lack of ambition. It is a question of mentality and behaviors across the organizations. If companies want to promote women, they have to adapt their ways of working, their management style—really it is a true cultural change that companies have to undertake.

> If companies want to promote women, they have to adapt their ways of working, their management style.

But I am very optimistic that more and more companies will go that way. However, we men and women have to support gender equality across company organizations because, in the end, it will be positive for us all.

What made you decide to become a mentor?

I have been lucky, throughout my career path, to meet quite a few people who have helped me grow and improve myself, so it was time for me now to do the same and give back! Being a mentor is not only a great opportunity for the mentee. It is also a wonderful opportunity for me to meet new people, new ways of thinking. It is first of all a win-win relationship. And I enjoy it.

How many mentees have you supported?

I have had two mentees so far. I completed one mentoring a few months ago. We met six or seven times over the year. It was pretty unique because my mentee, Paola Vezzaro, was promoted to Thailand (from Italy) during the course of her mentoring. We managed to see each other once physically in Paris and then through visio-conferences between Paris and Bangkok.

How did the mentoring with Paola go?

Mentoring Paola was really interesting. Paola is an experienced woman with an impressive background. At first sight, you would not think she needs mentoring at all due to her career path so far. But Paola was a newcomer within ENGIE, and she needed to learn how to adapt to a bigger organization, to improve her communication skills (to better formalize her requests, for example), to understand the culture of the company, and to improve her network. *What is important to understand is that mentoring is NOT a career accelerator for the mentee*: it is first of all a way to understand the company culture and organization better, to improve one's own behavior and learn how to adapt, and to progress within the organization. Mentors are here to help and make the mentees grow. Mentors are not here to promote them.

I am also in the process of mentoring another woman. We are at the beginning. Paola and my new mentee have different backgrounds and expectations, but they have this true willingness to better understand the organization of ENGIE, and to make sure they will do things right. They both have a real sense of ethics and share common values. It is really important.

What does the mentoring experience bring to you?

Working for many years now at the ENGIE headquarters, mentoring for me is really refreshing. It is really important to keep contact with the business field. It is a little time-consuming, but if you want to have results, you have to show commitment. It is for me an opportunity to give—but also receive. The sharing experience is really important. What strikes me is that the mentees often point out things that I was not aware of, or I did not see anymore (probably because I've been with ENGIE for many years now!).

What advice would you give to a woman employee seeking promotion to key posts of responsibility? Or interested in participating in a mentoring program?

First of all: **Believe in yourself!** I am always surprised by women's lack of confidence in themselves.

Second**: Dare!** Women should dare to ask for promotion even if they feel that the job is not for them! Do it! Otherwise no one will come to you.

Third: **Trust!** I believe that women's positions will improve because men will understand that it is important for everyone within the organization. It is not women against men—but men with women—who must work to achieve this cultural change.

My final advice: Enroll now in a mentoring program. It is a great opportunity!

INTERVIEW WITH PAOLA VEZZARO (MENTEE)

> Know what you are looking for in the mentoring program, because the selection of the mentor is also key.

Paola has worked with ENGIE since 2011, first as HR and Organization Director in Italy, and, since June 2014, as head of HR Asia Pacific. She has been a mentee in the ENGIE Mentoring Program since January 2014.

Can you tell me briefly about your business career?

I have two degrees, the first one in business administration and the second one in political science. I have always worked in multinationals. The first part of my career, for 10 years, was outside of HR, in marketing and sales, customer relations, and finance. And the second part was 10 years in HR, as head of HR in different sectors. The main companies I worked for were Xerox, Barclays, and now ENGIE.

Do you feel there are any obstacles to women achieving key posts of responsibility within companies?

I think there has been a big change over the years. I started to work in American companies, and there were policies in terms of diversity management, and that was important. But in some countries, it was not the same. Policies are important to make people think about employment processes. In Europe the focus was more on gender balance and also the sense that there was the necessity of some key elements, such as processes of support. When I was in Xerox, for example, there was a fast-track policy—I was part of the fast track—high-potential people—not because I was a woman. But then, later on, I was the only woman on the board, and it was not so easy. In Barclays, we're talking about after 2000, when it was already known that it was better to have more than one woman on the board, I had the experience of being one of two women. There was a very senior manager who was from America, who was a woman, and who was very supportive. So: processes, senior people who are part of the company and support the principle from a different perspective, and, in ENGIE, it's even better because we have a man, Gérard Mestrallet, who promotes a gender balance of women and communicates it. So, there were obstacles, but now it's much better.

The sector is less important than the policies and the belief of the CEO. Because, for example, in L'Oreal, I expect it could be easier for a woman to take a senior position due to the business. Here, in the energy sector, one can think that it's more difficult, but in reality, in the next few weeks, we are going to have a woman CEO because there is a belief. So in ENGIE there are people, there are processes, there are resources, and there is a belief in gender diversity. The next step that we should do here is to stress that gender balance is important; we should improve it but in an inclusive way—so it's not a question of "more women—less men"; it's a question of good balance between the two—and this is the next step for ENGIE, I think.

Why did you apply for a mentoring program?

Because in general, as a person, I like to consult with other people; I learn from other people; I like to share my opinion and get feedback and others' points of view. So you can have counsellors, you can have coaches, and you can have mentors. The difference with the mentor is that the mentor is a person that knows the organization that you work in. As I joined ENGIE in 2011, it was important for me to have someone who could help me in understanding the logic of ENGIE, which, as you know, is a French company—yes, a multinational, but a French company. So that is why I asked for a mentor.

I joined the mentoring program in January of 2014; officially, it lasts one year but due to the fact that you build—or at least I have built—a good relationship with my mentor, the relationship can last longer than one year. So, for example, next week I will go to Paris because we have a big convention, and my mentor is based in Paris and so I will meet him.

What were your needs when you joined the mentoring program?

Exactly what I said to you, and it was also formalized; I don't know if you are aware, but in ENGIE, mentoring is very well structured. So there is a kick-off where the processes are explained to you, what you can get, what to do. So, for example, they suggest you write down and agree with your mentor your objectives, then write down your reflections after your different meetings with your mentor, and I followed these suggestions to make my mentoring more successful. So I can tell you the objectives that I wrote, questions I asked to my mentor. They were:

- What are the do's and don'ts in ENGIE?
- What are the main similarities and differences between French culture and Italian culture that I should be aware of?
- What are the main policies it's important for me to know—not the formal ones but the informal ones?

So those were the objectives. During the year there was the event related to my move to Bangkok. In the beginning I was head of HR in an organization in Europe—in Italy. And then I moved here to Bangkok—and in fact I moved in June last year. So what happened is that my mentor helped me before and after to reflect, and, if you want, he was close to me in my move. So, to give you an example: before I moved, he gave me some information about my future manager—the one that I found here in Bangkok. And after, when I came here, he made a sort of checking point— he asked me, "Is everything okay? Did you get the support from the group?" So this was something that happened that was not in the plan at the beginning.

What were the aspects which had the most impact on your business career?

The mentor has had no influence on my move, because this was based on other HR processes. What was really important is that now that I am in Bangkok, I am very far from Paris, but my mentor, who works in the headquarters and at group level, helps me if I need anything related to the figures of the group or this kind of thing. So he's the one who can give me what I need at the strategic level.

How would you assess the mentoring experience? How did it benefit you?

I think, in my work, the information that he gave me—related to the people that I was going to find here—helped me to be success- ful from the very beginning in my new job. So this is something for sure I can say. And the second one is that I think I feel very lucky to have a link with the group, even though I'm very far from Paris. Because for my job and in my style of management, I really need to be close to the main strategic elements of the group—to the head of the company.

What advice would you give to a woman employee seeking promotion to key posts of responsibility? Or interested in participating in a Mentoring Program?

For sure, mentoring is one of the elements, but I don't suggest women to ask for a mentor in order to improve their career. The improvement in terms of career is more than that. But for sure, a mentor can help you—and give you some information—that you cannot get in other ways.

> Know what you are looking for in the mentoring program, because the selection of the mentor is also key.

So yes, I would suggest asking for a mentor, and I also would suggest knowing what you are looking for in the mentoring program, because the selection of the mentor is also key. So when I asked to be part of the mentoring program, and they said yes, they asked me to fill out a document and they asked me the objectives and the characteristics of the mentor I would love to have. They didn't guarantee, but there was an opportunity—and I was clear that I needed someone from the group—and I got it.

"Mentoring" is a word that is used very often, but there are different levels of maturity in order to implement and get value from mentoring. Sometimes, even if the process is not well structured, if you are lucky, and you get a good mentor, you can benefit. But if a company really not only selects people and makes a mentoring pair but has a process and supports the process, it is then an organizational process that is very well known and adds value itself.

So, in summary, you can have examples of mentoring, or you can have a mentoring organizational process. In ENGIE we have the second one.

17

Oracle

> When you do ... something extraordinary, when you do something that is beyond your normal responsibility, do a great job and tell people about it, talk about it to the people who can influence your career.

Nicoleta has worked at Oracle Romania since April 2008, as Senior Technology Consultant, Pre-Sales Team Leader, and Sales Consulting Manager. She is responsible for leadership of projects and teams, people management, recruitment, performance management, remote management, and demand generation. She has been in the Oracle mentoring program since October 2014 and was scheduled to finish the program in June 2015.

Can you tell me briefly about your business career?

I'm a techie girl. I studied computer science, did Java programming before joining Oracle as a technology consultant, and took the role of a technical architect in Oracle for two years and half. Ever since high school, I've always known what I wanted: I've always seen myself as a people-oriented person—but also good at mathematics, informatics, with technical ability. So I pursued an IT career, but always knew that, by the age of 30, I wanted to be a people manager—a combined business-oriented and people-management role. For the last three years I've been managing teams across multiple physical locations. I manage local and remote teams, which is more complex, but it has definitely brought me a lot of learning. To summarize, I'm a technology specialist with a people-oriented approach. Business is important, of course, but business is made with people. So I try to put people first.

Do you feel there are any obstacles to women achieving key posts of responsibility, particularly within the tech industry?

During my studies, more than ten years ago, there was an initiative for the ladies to do some IT courses that, initially, men didn't have access to, with the intention to promote women in IT. Nowadays, in the organization and team that I am part of, there is no difference between men and women. Women have the same level of responsibilities, rights, everything—every opportunity is the same for a man and a woman.

> In the broader IT world, the majority is comprised of men, and it takes much more time and effort for a woman as an IT professional or IT manager to build her personal brand and receive recognition.

But in the broader IT world, I feel that, in general, the majority is comprised of men, and it takes much more time and effort for a woman as an IT professional or IT manager to build her personal brand and receive recognition, in front of a group mainly formed by men. I've been in different situations where I had senior management comprised of men, and I was, at the beginning of my management career, a young woman, presenting in front of them, promoting my team or sometimes having more difficult conversations—it was not easy because I was young, I was a woman, a Romanian, etc. I've been here for seven years, growing professionally from Java developer, technical consultant, technical architect, and manager. Throughout this time I've invested in my development, time, effort, I've done an MBA as well—because I wanted to expand my knowledge on other non-IT areas such as finance, accounting, marketing, HR. The MBA gave me management knowledge from a business point of view—different lines of businesses and what they do. And I was lucky to have my management team's support to pursue the MBA studies.

Can you tell me about the mentoring you have received?

The mentoring is part of a cross-company mentoring program that Oracle Women's Leadership Group has developed with other companies on the market. I was one of the three mentees selected from Oracle, and I have a mentor from a company from a different industry—not an Oracle partner, nor a competitor. I found the mentee pairing was an excellent match in my case. My mentor is a woman, she leads an organization of more than 1,200 people, and she is a great inspiration for me.

Why did you apply for a mentoring program?

I wanted to get more exposure to a different industry, and learn from the experience of a senior leader. As a middle-level manager, I'm focused on the operations, but I wanted to get insights into a more strategic level, or how to manage managers, for example.

Did you have any preparation before beginning the mentoring program?

There was no official course. We have the HR team coordinating and helping the mentees and mentors. These great ladies are the drivers of the program. We had initial meetings, where we set the expectations and received materials to guide us through this program: how to set objectives, how to meet, when to meet. They touch base with us regularly to ask, "How is it going? Do you need additional support?" or give advice.

How did the first meeting with your mentor go?

It was very open. I was surprised by the friendly atmosphere and the openness of my mentor. At the same time, I was a bit shy about expressing all my needs from the beginning, because the first meeting was still getting to know each other and to see if our personalities match—but in the second meeting, I needed her help. At that time I was direct in expressing my current challenges at work, said exactly what I needed from her as mentor, and that basically cracked the ice.

How long is the mentoring?

It is about six months; I am still in the program. It started in October, and it's going to finish in June. We try to meet every month—we have face-to-face meetings once a month, and we decided to communicate through email and over the phone—we plan to do that on video Skype as well.

What were the aspects that have had the most impact on your business career?

Receiving insight and the perspective of how things are running in another multinational corporation, but in a totally different industry. And at the same time to see how a leader of 1,200 people operates: from communication to leading a management team from a more strategic point of view and learning from her experience.

How would you assess the mentoring experience?

It is beneficial if you know when and how to use it.

First and most important is the Goal. *Know what you want. Where do you want to go? What is your goal?*

Second: *Go beyond*—go beyond your responsibilities, be proactive, take initiatives, take leadership.

And third is about visibility: when you do something, something extraordinary, talk about it to the people who can influence your career.

The "when" is critical—choose carefully when you decide to do this in your career. I've been meaning to do this for the last three years, and now I realize that three years ago it would have brought nothing to me; now is the time in my career when I am facing a real need and seek guidance, perspectives, experience.

What advice would you give to a woman employee seeking promotion to key posts of responsibility? Or interested in participating in a mentoring program?

I see three areas in terms of career promotion.

First and most important is the Goal. *Know what you want. Where do you want to go? What is your goal?* and *In how much time do you want to achieve this goal? Know what you want and by when.*

Second: *Go beyond*—go beyond your responsibilities, be proactive, take initiatives, take leadership, expose yourself to situations where you learn something: if you stay in your corner and just do your standard job, you will learn nothing. *Be yourself*—be you as a manager; be natural, because people feel that.

And the third is about visibility: when you do something, something extraordinary, when you do something that is beyond your normal responsibility, do a great job and tell people about it, talk about it to the people who can influence your career. Otherwise, if you just do it, but nobody knows about it, nothing will happen. Make sure that your work has an impact that is beneficial to others. I'm often told, "Make yourself visible; you're doing such great work but people don't know about it, so tell them—otherwise how can you be promoted in the future?"

From a mentoring perspective, the first advice is timing. Choose the timing in your career for a mentoring program wisely; it is critical. Secondly, make sure that you identify one or two areas where you want to develop—but be specific, be realistic, set yourself a SMART objective, don't have more than two areas, maximum three if you can cope with that, because the mentoring will not have a clear focus, and it will not bring any real benefit.

———

INTERVIEW WITH GIOVANNA SANGIORGI (MENTOR)

The top advice is: one, look for a sponsor and the other is to speak out about your leadership ambition, don't be afraid of that.

Giovanna is vice president at Oracle Direct EMEA. She has an in-depth knowledge of the IT market and has developed management expertise in complex and multicultural organizations. She has wide experience in sales, operations, and back office organizations and processes. Her career development has been based on integrity, mutual respect, co-operation, and innovation, and she attributes her professional success to her focus, passion, and dedication.

Giovanna currently mentors five women in Oracle, both within the formal Oracle mentoring program and informally with women who have participated in the program but continue to benefit from Giovanna's support.

I see you currently mentor five women in Oracle—how does this work?

Probably this goes back to the fact that I am personally passionate about people, their development, and their careers. I'm really open to giving any kind of help or feedback to, let's say, younger people in general, and obviously many younger women see me as a sort of example.

> Mentoring quickly turns into a life-long relationship.

Since they have easy access to me, even if we start with a very formal mentorship program with some specific objectives, then this mentoring quickly turns into a life-long relationship, and randomly, not in a predefined way, they come to me not only to get advice but really to ask for help for specific things and objectives.

Can you tell me briefly about your business career?

This is the most difficult part of the interview! Probably I took risks and embraced every opportunity with focus and dedication. This is also what I usually say when talking about leadership with our top talented people: keep your eyes open to see opportunities, take some risks with passion, and work hard to make your value stand out.

I have been in IT for 30 years and have developed a broad spectrum of experiences. I started as a consultant, and then I moved into completely different positions—from purely technical roles to sales roles, and from sales roles to back office roles, and then back to sales. So, a very broad spectrum of different experiences but two constant elements. I've always been in IT and, at least for the past 18 years, leading international teams with broad multicultural dimensions.

> There are evident obstacles and I will summarize them: the first one, and probably the most difficult one, is ourselves.
>
> The second obstacle is that men are very protective of their privilege. That's why having a male sponsor may pay off.

I think I took my first international leadership position between 18 and 19 years ago, and since then, I've carried on with different kinds of responsibility—but always with a multinational, international team. I currently lead the "Inside Sales" organization for Europe, the Middle East, and Africa, and this includes demand generation and sales functions for all our business lines, six sites from Dublin to Dubai and more than 30 nationalities, every religion and belief, and I believe I am right in saying there is almost no manager in my organization who leads a team of people with the same nationality.

You've always worked in the IT sector; do you feel there are any obstacles to women achieving key posts of responsibility within the IT sector?

I would say yes—there are evident obstacles, and I will summarize them: the first one, and probably the most difficult one, is ourselves—more frequently than expected we are the first obstacles to our own career development. The thing is that we are not brought up to accept our career and leadership ambitions as normal, and this is due to a nurtured gender difference. We "unconsciously" feel guilty about feeding our leadership and power ambitions. I have a 20-year-old daughter and, while many may think this is a view from the past, I can tell you that is still surprisingly true also for many of the young generation today.

The IT environment is very male dominated — and this is the second obstacle. Despite the fact that we have seen a growing number of women taking chief executive positions, the IT sector remains male dominated and men are very protective of their privilege. That's why having a male sponsor may pay off.

What made you decide to become a mentor?

I would say it is much more to do with giving back. Probably, I was not really aware of that when I started, but now, after a few years of regularly mentoring people, I would say that it is really about giving back. It is a sort of mission for me to help and challenge women to feel really comfortable with their leadership and power ambitions. Helping them to feel comfortable and also be able to speak out about their ambition.

You are currently mentoring a number of women. Do you see any differences between them, or do they all want the same kind of thing?

It is really individual, and the culture plays a role in defining the differences. I hate to generalize, but it is common in some cultures to come to mentoring with clear objectives and a very well-structured career plan. Other people approach their career progression in a less structured way, so it is more common that they just seek advice. Others just come for help with specific identified issues.

What does the mentoring experience bring to you?

First it helps me to know myself better, knowing better what I'm good at. Whatever your business responsibility, whenever it comes to leadership, the more you know yourself and why you are a good leader, the better it is.

My first advice is look for a sponsor in the male world and ensure he is a true supporter of your career progression. My second is don't be afraid to speak out about your ambition.

I definitely found that the mentorship experience is a great experience in helping me know myself better. Obviously, it is time consuming — it is not just the time of the calls or the meeting, but also the preparation that each meeting requires. I try to be as inspirational as possible, so every meeting requires time.

What advice would you give to a woman employee seeking promotion to key posts of responsibility?

My first advice is look for a sponsor in the male world and ensure he is a true supporter of your career progression. My second is don't be afraid to speak out about your ambition. So if you want to get more responsibility, go and present yourself—be open in saying what is your ambition—let your manager know what you are looking for, let them know what you can offer and what makes you good at doing that job, and let them know what motivates you.

Another thing that prevents us from taking more of the promotion opportunities is that men apply for jobs even when they are only 80 percent ready, while women don't apply—unless we are 125 percent ready. So develop your confidence, don't be shy of your ambition, and speak out about it.

> Men apply for jobs even when they are only 80 percent ready, while women don't apply—unless we are 125 percent ready. So develop your confidence, don't be shy of your ambition, and speak out about it.

INTERVIEW WITH PAULA CRAYTHORNE (MENTEE)

> Continually grow your network and when you're doing that, demonstrate your value as an employee.

Paula is Senior Director of Business Development at Oracle. She has worked in various positions at Oracle since 1994. She has the experience of working in the East and Central Europe, Middle East and Africa regions, and her skills include business planning and analysis, program management, market strategy, CRM (Customer Relationship Management), and sales operations.

Can you tell me briefly about your business career?

I joined Oracle in 1994; I really enjoyed my job, but within around six months, I was thinking to myself, *Is this really what I want to do for the rest of my life?* I wanted to understand a bit more about how the company worked—and an opportunity came up to work in the commissions and bonuses department, and I applied for the position and was successful, and that exposed me to the sales teams where I learned about the products that Oracle sold and language and references that I'd never heard of before. After a couple of years, I moved on, and I was working first in an EMEA (Europe–Middle East–Africa)-wide role and then specifically for East and Central Europe soon after a new manager joined the management team, and although he's not officially a mentor of mine, he's had a big influence on me and my career and is one of the reasons why I'm in the job I'm in today. He's given me opportunities to learn and grow in the years that followed.

Do you feel there are any obstacles to women achieving key posts of responsibility, particularly within tech companies?

No I don't think so. I've only got the experience of Oracle—but I don't think that there are any obstacles. If you demonstrate that you're competent, if you demonstrate your desire and your ambitions to try different things, to do different jobs, to move around the organization, I don't think there are any obstacles that stop you—gender doesn't come into the equation.

Why did you apply for a mentoring program?

I went on a training course at Oracle for potential future leaders—and a recommendation from that program was to find a mentor if you didn't already have one. At that time, I didn't have an official mentor, but I discussed with my line manager whether I needed a mentor and what that person would do for me, and how that person would help me, and we decided it was somebody who could help me with my career progression in addition to being someone that I could bounce ideas off or ask advice from.

For example, maybe you're asked to run a project or a specific task—and it's new to you—and you can say to them, "Well, these are the ideas I have and how I want to approach it." And because they're more senior in the organization with more experience, it is valuable to get their feedback on your ideas and approach, and maybe they know somebody who could help you with expertise in that particular area so you are utilizing their network; you're extending your network through them.

> I discussed with my line manager whether I needed a mentor and what that person would do for me … and we decided it was somebody who could help me with my career progression.

What were your needs when you started the mentoring?

I think for me personally I was relatively new to the role I'm doing now, it was a shift, and I felt I was constantly learning—which was a good thing—but sometimes I was asked to do things, and I was thinking, *Okay, I really have to sit down and think. Where do I go? What's my starting point?* Thinking of what approach I would take, it was nice to be able to talk that through with somebody who was more expert in that field as well as more experienced in general. Somebody I could get some ideas off or share what I was doing with my work but also, like I say, using their network. Someone who could champion me [so] that when opportunities that they were aware of because of their position [came up], they could say, *Hey, do you know what? I know somebody who would be interested in that or who would be a good fit for that role.* Someone to sponsor me with more senior management.

Did you have any preparation or follow a course before beginning?

No, the mentor I have today is not through an official program. It's something that came out of this leadership training.

How did the first meeting with your mentor go?

It went well. We laid down the ground rules, and we both said how we wanted the relationship to work so it was very clear from the outset. We didn't set definitive timelines that we'd meet, for example, once a month or once every two weeks, but I told him what I was looking for from him. He agreed to that, and he said that was fine and that's how he saw the relationship working. We agreed on housekeeping, confidentiality, and such things, and even if there was something which did relate, in some way, back to him or his team, I always felt that he was very open to me being transparent, and I knew that what I'm saying stays within those four walls. Setting those boundaries is important at the beginning; as a mentee it is good to be reassured.

How long did the mentoring last?

It's been two and a half years.

What were the aspects that had the most impact on your business career?

> Networking for me is a big part of career progression: the more people you know, the more opportunities you're going to hear about.

There have been a couple of occasions where I've met with him, and I've felt, for varying reasons, in not such a good place about work. It's been good to talk that through with someone. Sometimes it's made me realize that maybe I'm reading a situation wrong or I'm overanalyzing something, and I've come away feeling better, thinking *Yes, maybe I was too quick to judge on a situation*. And I think access to the network. Networking for me is a big part of career progression: the more people you know, the more opportunities you're going to hear about, and the more people to whom you can demonstrate the value that you bring, the more opportunities that creates for you.

Do you belong to one or more professional or personal networks?

The majority of my networks are informal; I belong to the Oracle Women's Leadership here in the UK. They run sessions—not just for women—and have all sorts of different speakers come in, to talk about different topics. We had an ex-Olympic rower who came to talk to us about her achievements in the boat, and how that can transition across to business. We've had internal speakers as well, so you get to hear more about different parts of the Oracle strategy or particular areas of business that you might not get to hear about through your daily work. The OWL (Oracle Women's Leadership) group is very good, and I was fortunate enough last year to go to the headquarters in San Francisco where there's a two-day Global OWL event that opened up my network to people at corporate and also in other parts of the world that I don't normally interact with.

What advice would you give to a woman employee seeking promotion to key posts of responsibility? Or interested in participating in a mentoring program?

Continually grow your network, and when you're doing that, demonstrate your value as an employee—also make sure you are clear on your brand and articulate that when you meet with someone for the first time. Demonstrating your value and making sure that people know what your key competences are and what you're about, what your brand is, is key. I believe mentoring is also important: if you want somebody to help you in your career progression, then approach someone who is in that position to help you, and do not be frightened to change your mentor if your circumstances change or if their circumstances change.

18

Publicis Groupe

> Mentoring...makes me look at things from a different perspective.

Michele is executive vice president and managing director of Global P&G at Leo Burnett Worldwide, a subsidiary of Publicis Groupe.

You have had a long and brilliant career in advertising....

Yes, that's true! I started out at Benton & Bowles in New York as media director for Procter & Gamble and then moved to Saatchi & Saatchi in Paris at the beginning of the 1990s. After Saatchi & Saatchi, I moved to the McCann agency before joining D'Arcy, Paris, where I was responsible for international management, with all its challenges—a position that suited me very well! Following the merger, I ended up in Publicis Groupe in 2002 and was appointed Managing Director / Global Head of P&G Surface Care Leo Burnett Paris, and member of the agency's management committee—and in 2010, was appointed Global Lead P&G

Leo Burnett Worldwide, and, consequently, became part of the Chicago head office management team.

Why did you decide to become a mentor?

VivaWomen!—Publicis' internal mentoring network—is the only network I'm part of, and I believe it's important to share our experiences with younger women, so that they can understand how to develop their career in our sector.

> It's important to share our experiences with younger women so that they can understand how to develop their career in our sector.

This is not always an easy thing to do—but it's always exciting! As an American, even if I've been in France now for 20 years, I'm used to this type of network, and it's great to see it developing among the women in our group.

Did you receive any training before you started mentoring?

We had half a day's training, which enabled us to define what mentoring is within Publicis, and what it isn't. It is not counseling nor a place to let out your emotions! And we mentors are not the Human Resources department! What it is, is a sharing of experiences where the most experienced of the pair (the mentor) can bring a different perspective to help the mentee develop her career.

How did you choose your mentee?

The match between Charlotte Guillabert and myself was made by the program team according to the questions that Charlotte was asking and the topics that I had identified as good for me. At our first meeting, we agreed on the rules of engagement, so that everything was clear from the start. We also asked other questions, such as What were the goals of the mentoring process? How often would we meet? Where would we meet? Who would be responsible for what? How would we manage our relationship between meetings? How long would the mentoring last (three, six, or 12 months)? In the end, the mentoring lasted six months, which seemed the right amount of time to both of us.

What were the highlights for you?

I think that talking to someone who can see the bigger picture relieves the anxiety and stress that you might feel when you begin to question yourself. And sharing experiences was a good way to help Charlotte to find her route through difficult situations.

What do you think about it now—in retrospect?

It was a great experience on both a human and professional level. My only regret is that Charlotte and I weren't able to have a formal end to the relationship because of my sudden move to the United States! It would have been good to review the relationship together, look back on how far she had come, and look to the future to see where she might go. We're going to do it anyway—later on, and that will also give us some time for reflection ... for me, I'd like to continue mentoring because it's not only useful for the mentee, but useful for the mentor too; it makes me look at things from a different perspective.

INTERVIEW WITH CHARLOTTE GUILLABERT (MENTEE)

Listen to your mentor and use her experience.

Charlotte is International Account Manager, Sanofi, at Publicis Conseil, a subsidiary of Publicis Groupe.

How did you get to where you are now?

I joined Publicis in 2007 as international knowledge manager for the Sanofi account team. The post had just been created in order to share information across a number of countries (67 in the case of Sanofi, which was my account) through digital asset management tools. In 2012, I changed jobs—still within the same team—and became International Account Manager. I look after Sanofi's regional and global clients, especially the Consumer Healthcare division and Pet Health, and I work to develop their advertising campaigns with our agencies within the group.

Why did you apply to the mentoring program?

In a major group such as Publicis, there are a lot of talented people, but it's not always easy to get in touch with them because we're all very involved with our daily jobs. When I learned that VivaWomen!, the internal network that I'm part of, was launching a mentoring program, I thought it would be a great opportunity to meet someone with more experience who could advise me on my career development. So I didn't hesitate to apply. It was a real opportunity to get some advice on my career.

What were you looking for?

First of all, I wanted to have a discussion about my career development—to get some advice to help me to make the right decisions; secondly, I wanted to hear about how a more senior woman had got to the position she had. I wanted to benefit from the support of a mentor who managed an international account. VivaWomen! looked for such a person for me, and it turned out to be Michele Gilbert. Before starting, I prepared a few questions for our first meeting. I wanted it to be as natural as possible and that, together, we'd decide on the range of topics for our subsequent meetings.

What were the highlights for you?

Michele and I immediately got on well together. We talked about our professional experiences, then listed the points where I needed some advice. The whole experience turned out to be hugely beneficial for my career, but if I had to choose one thing, it would be Michele's participation in a workshop I had organized for my client in which together we led an afternoon's topic on "creative debriefing."

What do you think about it now—in retrospect?

The mentoring lasted six months. There weren't any difficulties— only positives! Overall, mentoring was a great experience.

I increased my confidence and learned a lot about myself—both on a professional and on a personal level.

> Mentoring was a great experience. I increased my confidence and learned a lot about myself—both on a professional and on a personal level.

I got answers to the questions I wanted to ask, which enabled me to develop both in the short term and in the longer term. I would recommend that any woman interested in doing something similar should do it—and to do anything they can to have a similar experience. Don't hesitate to open yourself up, to ask questions, even if they seem simplistic, and above all, listen to your mentor and use her experience.

19

BNY Mellon

Certainly mentoring is front and center.

Regina ("Regi") is executive vice president and chief operating officer for The Markets Group, which includes Foreign Exchange, Securities Finance, Capital Markets, Collateral Management, and Prime Brokerage. She is also responsible for the regional management in EMEA and APAC (Asia Pacific).

Previously, Regi served as chief administrative officer of BNY Mellon's Financial Markets & Treasury Services (FMTS), where she managed a team that established best practices across the group and executed initiatives in various disciplines, including Communications, Employee Engagement, Marketing & Market Research, Sales Planning & Development, and Learning & Development. Before FMTS, Regi served in the UK as asset servicing CAO, responsible for global strategy, quality assurance, facilities management, and budget planning, as well as learning and development. She also was the primary interface with corporate business partners, including Communications, Human Resources, Legal, Accounting, Risk, and Compliance.

During the previous seven years, while in London, Regi held several positions, including head of European Client Management and head of Country Management for Europe. She was a member of the EMEA Executive Committee, European Risk Committee, and co-chair of the global Investment Services Client Engagement Steering Committee. She was also a director of BNY Holding Limited, a member of the BNY Hamilton Funds Board, and also a member of The Prince's Trust Women's Leadership Group.

Regi is a member of BNY Mellon's Operating Committee and the Global Diversity Council. She is an active member of WIN and is co-chair of the Executive Committee of BNY Mellon's Women's Initiative Network (WIN). For its success in promoting the advancement of women in the company, the leaders of BNY Mellon's WIN were named a Top Team (2009) by *American Banker* magazine/*US Banker*, as part of the annual review of the most powerful women on Wall Street.

Since 2009, BNY Mellon has witnessed a significant increase in the number of women and people from a diverse ethnic background on the Executive Committee, Operating Committee, and Regional Operating Committee levels. Forty-four percent of the global workforce are women; 36 percent of the VPs are women; 26 percent of the MDs are women; and 19 percent of the Executive Committee are women.

How do you see the role of women in today's economic/financial world?

Women obviously play a very important role in the economy. My specific comments will be focused on the financial industry, since this is where I have spent all of my career. According to a recent Gallup poll regarding the financial services sector, 60 percent of the workers are women, but as you move up the corporate hierarchy of these firms, only 19 percent make it in senior leadership roles, 14 percent have a seat on the board, and only 2 percent are CEOs. Although we have a lot of Woman Power in the industry, they are not high enough in these organizations to bring about needed change. We still have a lot of work to do in this sector.

Do you think women managers bring any particular advantages to the company? If so, what?

Our Pershing organization recently launched a White Paper on the different characteristics of male vs. female managers. Although one should not generalize, male management characteristics tend to be more top down, authoritarian, commanding, and controlling while women focus more on building a collaborative environment, emphasizing team work, and building a consensus, so that their teams will own the decision and its outcome. Having this male/female diversity in management gives you a 360-degree view of your options and should allow you to make better decisions.

What are the major obstacles that prevent women from attaining key decision-making posts?

During my 37 years in the industry, there has been an evolution in women's roles. I actually don't believe there are as many barriers as people write about. Develop the right foundation early in your career. As an example, it is important to have experience in how to manage a budget, run a sales team, and learn management techniques so that you will be equipped to run a business. Running a business is an important stepping stone for an Executive Management position down the road. Women more often gravitate towards support/staff functions, and no matter how senior they are this rarely leads to the C-Suite.

> Develop the right foundation early in your career.... Network better.... It is all about getting to know the influencers in your company/industry and creating the exposure with management so that you will be considered for the next job.

Network better, but on your own terms. If you want to leave "on time" to care for your family, then think about alternative activities, like lunches, that can reap the same benefits. It is all about getting to know the influencers in your company/industry and creating the exposure with management, so that you will be considered for the next job.

In summary, it is learning financial/quantitative skills early in your career and having exposure so that you can showcase these skills.

What advice/support can we give to women to overcome these obstacles?

First, it is awareness raising—realizing that there are obstacles that you need to overcome or, more importantly, skills you need to develop. It is not "complaining why you didn't get that promotion," but understanding what qualifications you need to be considered and advertising that you have them.

What we did in WIN to assist the development of these skills is launch a financial acumen training program through a series of webcasts taught by executives in the firm. Once completed, this gave the participants a comfort level of the subject matter; and therefore, we used training to overcome the obstacle.

The other area of development—networking and exposure—this is one of the tremendous advantages of WIN, which allows you to network on multiple levels and "practice being a leader" at the WIN committee level. Because senior men are part of our events and activities, it provides a unique exposure opportunity.

Within the WIN network, do you run a mentoring program?

The WIN organization is a little more than 10 years old. Mentoring was the first program we created. In the United States, it was all women; in Europe it included men mentors. I was based in London at the inception of the program and started WIN EMEA, where we included men early on in an advisory capacity. The reason for taking this approach was due to guidance I received from other firms who had established Women's ERG's curve. We were advised to be inclusive or fail in Europe. This was a critical decision point, because in most cases men ran our biggest businesses in Europe, and by including them in the process we had their support to give our WIN women exposure they could not get in their day job. Executive men observing WIN members lead from all levels gave them recognition and exposure, so that they were better considered for the next promotion or assignment.

So at the very beginning, what was the purpose of the mentoring?

From the European context, we identified what women lacked in the workplace was exposure with NYC Executive Management, who made most career advancement decisions in those days. Many of our European women were in support infrastructure jobs and had the responsibility, but not the title that their position warranted. Some might call this a glass ceiling, but actually it was worse. They were in the job, just not recognized. This would ultimately lead to the "Leaking Pipeline" where women frustrated with the lack of advancement would leave. We used the mentoring program to help these women develop presentation and negotiation skills and to showcase them with executive management when they traveled from NYC.

> Today we are very conscious of the "Frozen Middle"—women who can't move past the middle-management level after child-bearing years.

Today we are very conscious of the "Frozen Middle"—women who can't move past the middle-management level after child-bearing years. They believe that they fall off the radar of top talent once they take their leave of absence. We are working on a support program to remedy this.

Anything you want to add?

Yes, you mentioned sponsoring vs. mentoring. We have a developed a robust mentoring program, but we are still working on our sponsoring program. The sponsor takes a risk on the sponsee, which is quite different from a mentoring relationship, which is one of guidance. Connecting these pairs (sponsor vs. sponsee) properly is critical for the success of the program. This is what we are working on now.

———

INTERVIEW WITH YOON PARK (REVERSE MENTOR)

> We have to be more confident, we have to know our work and know our worth.

Yoon is vice president, OTC Derivatives Regulatory Reform, BNY Mellon. Yoon has worked at BNY Mellon since September 2012 and is responsible for the implementation of Title 7 of the Dodd-Frank Act and EMIR with a focus on client communications and relationship management.

She is the mentor of Jeff Kuhn in the BNY Mellon WIN Reverse Mentoring Program.

Tell me a little about your career to date

After graduating from college with a BA in chemistry and economics, I thought I wanted to pursue a career in law, so I worked for about two years as a legal assistant, first at a large law firm, and then at a hedge fund in New York City. Then I went to law school, and after graduation, came to BNY Mellon about three years ago to join what we now call the OTC Derivatives Regulatory Reform Team. My role on the team is a perfect opportunity to combine my legal training with support for an important investment services business.

During this past year, I moved into my first position as a manager, and now I'm heading a newly created team. It's been a very challenging and rapidly evolving role, and I'm absolutely enjoying it.

Do you think there are any obstacles to women achieving posts of responsibility?

While growing up and attending school, I never felt that being a woman would stand in the way of achieving whatever I wanted to accomplish. Fortunately for me as a person, that thought never entered my mind.

> When women are supposed to be developing their careers, they're also dealing with the societal pressure and desire to find a partner and start a family.

That said, as my career has progressed, I've started to see the challenges of balancing work and life, fighting stereotypes, and changing longstanding cultural norms that are biased against women. I've become more aware of the importance of timing as a career factor. When women are in their late twenties and early thirties, the time in their lives when women are supposed to be developing their careers, they're also dealing with the societal pressure and desire to find a partner and start a family. The issues are real and, for me, might become personal as starting a family is something I don't want to compromise. In the next three, five, or ten years, I might be in a position where it would make sense to take a detour or make a lateral move to work on an aspect of my life other than my professional career.

Reverse mentoring: Why did you apply?

The easiest place to start is explaining why I *didn't* apply for my company's conventional mentoring program. I already had traditional mentoring relationships with my managers—I've been lucky enough to learn from and train under the company veterans, and this natural mentorship has been both effective and critical in my early career.

Our Reverse Mentoring Program gave me the opportunity to have an entirely different mentoring experience. I was invited to participate in our company's pilot program, and got paired with my mentee, Jeff, an executive who's distinguished himself as one of our resident continuous process improvement experts. Having a mentoring relationship with someone who's a member of the company's Operating Committee was one of those opportunities you just can't turn down. I'm glad I didn't. Thanks to the care with which the program's been designed and administered, it's provided a venue where I'm welcomed—even encouraged—to share observations and expectations from my vantage point.

What do you hope to gain from the Reverse Mentoring Program?

In my meetings with my mentee, we talk about my perspective as a millennial—what issues junior team members are facing, and what motivates and interests us. We talk about how management decisions are being perceived; cultural differences between senior management and junior employees; day-to-day issues I face at work, and how I approach them. Sharing my take on company decisions serves as a springboard for conversations about the company's bigger strategic initiatives and projects. Through open dialogue, I can offer my feedback and my perspective.

I'm relatively new to the industry, and I'm a working manager, so my focus tends to be up close and here and now. I'll take a deep dive into a particular issue at work, and Jeff will share with me a more strategic perspective on initiatives underway to address similar issues, and he'll ask for my opinion. Learning how to apply that kind of perspective—seeing things through a wide angle, wealth-of-know-how lens—that's what I seek from this program.

Did you have any preparation before you began the mentoring relationship?

The mentors met as a group beforehand to prepare for our first meeting with our mentees. One piece of advice was especially helpful: whether you're talking to a colleague, or your staff, your manager, or a client, you first have to establish a rapport based on confidence and trust. That was a helpful reminder that a mentoring relationship can't be forced: it has to be developed.

How did that first meeting with your mentee go?

My mentee was very open, much more approachable than I had imagined. He set the tone by letting me know that I was in charge of the conversation. He was all ears, eager to hear what I had to say, what ideas I had, and what I thought he could do to help effect change when change was appropriate. I really appreciated that.

What aspect of this reverse mentoring will have the most impact on your professional career?

I have an appreciation for the years of experience our senior management has invested in getting to where they are in their careers. They worked hard, and they've done something right. Just getting a glimpse of their path has been instructional and valuable. Every time I speak to my mentee, I feel reinvigorated, and have a sense that I can have an impact, no matter how small. Exposure to my mentee's level of management, leadership, and decision making has been invaluable. Plus, by interacting and engaging with someone at that level, I hope to gain a new level of composure and maturity that will help me grow professionally.

> Every time I speak to my mentee, I feel re-invigorated, and have a sense that I can have an impact, no matter how small.

What advice would you give to a woman who is trying to get to a more senior level?

First and foremost, know what you are capable of. Work really hard to become that go-to person, a subject matter expert. And don't be afraid to use your emotional intelligence and empathy that we have as women. Whenever I'm presenting an idea or making a decision, I always try to apply this combination—going with confidence, talking about what I believe in, sharing what I know.

Of course, women cannot overcome these challenges alone. So if you can, find a workplace, a group, a team, or a manager that is supportive. Change comes from efforts at every level, and I see many companies, like mine, making an effort to create more opportunities for women. Finally, be more confident. We have to know our work and know our worth, not apologize for being there. With that, we can achieve more.

INTERVIEW WITH JEFF KUHN (REVERSE MENTEE)

> You have to have very little fear but have confidence and go for it.

Jeff is executive vice president and one of the leaders of Client Service Delivery at BNY Mellon, where he has worked since 1998.

Jeff has been involved in BNY Mellon's WIN mentoring program for years, and is currently the reverse mentee of Yoon Park, Associate.

Can you tell me briefly about your business career?

I started in management consulting, but I had an opportunity to move into an internal consulting group at a money center bank. I ended up having many different roles, from securities operations to creating a precious metals depository to starting an electronics stock exchange. Immediately following 9/11, I was actively involved in the recovery of the bank and then contributing to the creation of public policy with the Federal Reserve.

So a lot of different roles—some by luck, some with a lot of careful thought of what would give me a broader set of experiences.

Do you feel there are any obstacles to women achieving key posts of responsibility within financial companies?

At BNY Mellon we do some fantastic work to promote careers for women, but if you look at the actual headcount, and the senior management, the gender split is not as rounded as even the bank would like. I don't think there are specific obstacles, but I think that there may be unconscious bias. At BNY Mellon, I don't see us differentiating between men, women, or minorities—I think we are very performance based. It's all about *can you deliver and execute against your task*?

We have become more focused on defining goals and your ability to achieve your goals. So from that perspective, there are no obstacles. There may be unconscious biases—implications to a woman's career if she chooses to go on maternity leave or have a different job because she's going to spend more time raising children. But I think those are challenges that society faces, and I think generally we're willing not to slow down a woman's career based on those things.

Tell me a little about mentoring at BNY Mellon, and particularly about the Reverse Mentoring Program and its goals.

The Reverse Mentoring Program is a way for more seasoned individuals to get to think about work and opportunities to make BNY Mellon, which is a traditional company, more appealing for the millennials. I see it as twofold: 1) it's an opportunity for me to understand what Yoon and her colleagues view as important at a traditional company versus an entrepreneurial startup: what types of things they are looking for and what challenges they are experiencing. And 2) it's about my learning what the challenges are, where I can help my mentor and apply that knowledge to other millennials and developing the talent in the company.

> The Reverse Mentoring Program is an opportunity to grow our high-end millennial talent.

The Reverse Mentoring Program is an opportunity to grow our high-end millennial talent. We were selective in choosing the individuals for the program, and I think it's very successful.

In terms of the institution, what will happen post Reverse Mentoring Program?

I suggested bringing a round table together to discuss lessons learned and opportunities going forward in the middle of the first year. And we're doing that.

What I use the information for is in thinking about how to recruit and how to run the job-rotation schemes in the operations area of the bank. With my colleagues, we manage an operation of about 18,000 people, and this is an excellent way to attract and maintain the best talent. So I think about my conversations with my mentor and her peers in terms of the strategies that we could take to address our talent goals.

What advice would you give to a woman employee seeking promotion to a key post of responsibility?

Good question. I'd start the conversation with trying to understand what the person wants to do with the next wave—or the next two waves—of her career. *Do you want to do something creative? Do you want to be managing large organizations? Are you fascinated by organizational design and the management of organizations? Do you want to be an individual contributor? Do you want to drive strategies for a company, or do you want to be in the weeds and operate a company?* Those are discussions I'd have with anybody whether they're early in their career or farther along.

Then based on that, I would explore opportunities with them that might either help them gain experience or set them up to be recognized in that space. When you're early in your career, you may not have a clue. So gaining experience in the operations can pay off later.

So it's about trying to get an understanding of what their interests are, and then trying to identify opportunities that give you the chance to expand on your specific interests.

Anything else you want to say to women seeking advancement?

When I started my career I was focused on setting goals and achieving them. I started at a junior level and paid my dues. Recently I met four highly successful women that each took their job opportunities and pursued them. One is a CEO of a PR firm, another is a recognized national news reporter, the other is a movie producer, and the other is a CEO of her fourth technology start-up. They're all very personable, knowledgeable, and don't see any barriers. They seem to just go for it. They're smart, they are aggressive yet they don't come across as aggressive, and they pursued a track and performed really well and kept getting recognized for newer and newer opportunities. I see this as a similar quality whether you're a man or a woman: you have to have a can-do attitude and the confidence to just go for it.

Part V

WAYS TO HELP ENTREPRENEURS TO SUCCEED

ENTREPRENEURSHIP IS INCREASINGLY RECOGNIZED AS A real opportunity for women in the new economy and a driver of economic growth: between 2002 and 2007, the number of women-owned businesses grew by 20 percent, whereas the growth in men-owned firms was 5.5 percent. Furthermore, the economic impact of women-owned businesses is just under $3 trillion annually in the United States, and creates 16 percent of all U.S. jobs. So the new economy clearly offers women great opportunities for entrepreneurship, but many women entrepreneurs say they feel isolated and lack networks, and that this slows down their business growth.

In Part V, we discuss three ways to help women entrepreneurs to success: mentoring and sponsoring, networking, and specifically designed training programs.

Mentoring and sponsoring have a positive impact on entrepreneurship, and nonprofits, such as the Women Business Mentoring Initiative (WBMI) in Europe, are beginning to make a difference. Emilie Creuzieux, entrepreneur and CEO of Monbento says that mentoring helps her to clarify the key challenges her company faces and to find her own solutions. Her mentor, Jean-Jacques Berard, co-founder of Executive Interim Management, believes that learning comes through talking with others, and this is where mentoring is important. For him, a company is about the 3Ps: product, people, and process, and he tells us how he helped Emilie to analyze her company using this simple formula. For Muriele Roos, founder of the women's magazine *Femme Majuscule*, mentoring gives her the energy to keep going in the face of difficult challenges.

Though not mentored through a structured program such as WBMI, U.S. entrepreneur Jane Chen, co-founder and CEO of Embrace, says that, in setting up a business, there are many tough moments when you just want to quit—and mentoring can help you through them. In a similar way, U.S. entrepreneur Clara Shih of Hearsay Social thinks that mentors and sponsors are important in helping women to lean in and take risks. For UK entrepreneur Abigail Holsborough of digital company RouteMap, one of the biggest obstacles is underselling herself when she needs to be out there pitching her business. She says that's when she needs her mentors—formal mentors to help her develop her pitching skills, identify the weak points in her strategy, and address her business needs—and informal mentors to address her personal needs for reassurance and confidence.

In addition to mentoring and sponsoring, networks are essential for support, for the sharing of business information, for gaining recognition, for marketing; indeed, being undernetworked can seriously slow down business growth. But women entrepreneurs lag behind in the networking stakes. Several reasons for this have been suggested in this book, but the view shared by everyone is that we need to change women's attitudes to networking if they are to achieve success. Two programs in particular illustrate the importance of professional networks: Dell's DWEN (Dell Women's Entrepreneur Network) and Astia.

DWEN brings together top global women entrepreneurs to share best practices, opportunities for international expansion, and new resources that support the growth of their businesses. The members stay connected through social networking sites and local events held throughout the world. Stephanie Cardot, founder and CEO of TO DO TODAY, says that she joined the network after 11 years of being an entrepreneur alone—and that reconnecting with other women entrepreneurs gave her the second wind that she needed to reboot her ambitions and vision.

Astia is a network that promotes high-growth women entrepreneurs: serial entrepreneurs, angel investors, venture capitalists, corporate leaders, bankers, accountants, and lawyers who all donate thousands of hours each year to the network.

In addition to these two professional networks, Goldman Sachs's 10,000 Women initiative was set up to support women entrepreneurs in developing countries by providing business and management education, mentors, networks, and links to capital. The results provide evidence that women can be successful entrepreneurs and that mentoring and networks are highly valued in the scaling-up process.

The third way to support women entrepreneurs is through specifically targeted training programs. In July 2015, Stanford Graduate School of Business delivered the first Women Entrepreneur Program, sponsored by BNP Paribas in conjunction with Women Business Mentoring Initiative. Programs such as these not only provide strategic insight and leadership training, but are also excellent networking opportunities.

Part V brings these three support strands together.

20

Mentoring and Sponsoring Programs

MENTORING WOMEN ENTREPRENEURS

The following pages describe a program aimed specifically at helping women launch, and then develop, their own companies: Women Business Mentoring Initiative (WBMI).

WBMI offers customized mentoring to women entrepreneurs. It was launched in September 2010 by Martine Liautaud and fellow alumni of the Stanford Graduate School of Business.

WBMI's founders had noticed that, among the various mentoring programs aimed at entrepreneurs in France, there was nothing specifically for women; and in particular, there was nothing for women facing the challenge of growing their companies.

Many entrepreneurs wind up their companies in the first three years, and those that continue need support to face the challenges of growth. WBMI's target is, therefore, women whose companies are more than three years old, and WBMI customizes its mentoring to support them through the challenges of growth.

There is only one criterion: the woman must have been an entrepreneur for more than three years. WBMI aims exclusively at women who set up, or took over, their companies at least three years previously, and offers them mentoring free of charge for a period of 9 to 12 months. WBMI has no other criteria for selecting its mentees, but recognizes that its mentoring is more useful if the company has a certain size; consequently, WBMI does not aim at freelancers or retail shops.

Mentors as Described by Mentees

WBMI consists of specialists from a range of professional backgrounds. They offer their advice free of charge and are able to put their mentees' companies and their needs into the bigger picture. The mentors provide a conceptual tool kit of skills and competences, access to their networks, advice in their respective professional areas, the sharing of experiences, and psychological and technical preparation for the next steps in the growth of the mentee's company. WBMI mentors are men and women who have succeeded in their own careers and who wish to give back to society for what they have received themselves.

In 2015, WBMI mentored its fourth cohort of mentees.

Since it was launched, WBMI has directly mentored 40 women entrepreneurs from a wide range of business sectors and with companies of various sizes from 1 million euros to 30 million euros turnover. Through its network of mentors/mentees, WBMI has also had an influence on more than 50 companies, which have benefited from one-off advice. In addition, six WBMI mentees have been chosen to represent young French entrepreneurs at the G20 YES (Young Entrepreneur Summit) in Mexico, Moscow, and Sydney.

Although their businesses are very different, the mentees all have strategic goals to achieve, which the mentors support and facilitate. WBMI's mentors can often provide a better media presence, access to networks (media, finance, law, human resources), and preparation for the important steps to be taken in the growth of the mentee's company.

With WBMI, each entrepreneur, whatever her company's phase of development, has been through one or more growth phases: strategic, operational, financial, and so on. With her mentor, she clarifies her company's goals, its organization, and its outlook, and each mentee says she feels better prepared to face the challenges of growth.

Partnerships to Increase Action

In order to sustain and strengthen its support for women entrepreneurs, WBMI has, from the very beginning, sought partnerships with major players in the economic and financial worlds.

Together with BNP Paribas, WBMI runs the Club des Entrepreneurs, which offers a hundred or so female CEOs topic-based practical seminars with well-known professionals on every aspect of a company's life.

To meet any needs entrepreneurs may have, BNP Paribas and WBMI have also written a handbook on women's entrepreneurship, *Entreprendre au feminin: mode d'emploi* (Female Entrepreneurship: A User's Guide) published by Eyrolles (2014).

With ENGIE, WBMI has initiated numerous projects to support both entrepreneurship and mentoring for women inside the ENGIE group.

In addition, WBMI is in partnership with Medef, Federation Pionnieres (France's number one incubator for women entrepreneurs), and Paris Initiative Entreprise (PIE), which is very active in financing start-ups and corporate buy-outs.

Finally, to promote women's entrepreneurship and broaden its scope, WBMI, together with ENGIE, sponsors a weekly TV show (on BFM Business) called *Ambitions d'entrepreneures* (Ambitions of Women Entrepreneurs), and also sponsors a Day of Women's Entrepreneurship with BNP Paribas.

Circle of Women Entrepreneurs

WBMI plans to scale up and expand its skills base by developing close links with major groups (in partnership or other types of relationship) in order to sustain the association and to strengthen its brand.

Because of its culture, its mentors' career backgrounds, and the size of its own network, WBMI is in a position to provide a link between major groups and the entrepreneurs it mentors (all cohorts included), as well as with the SMEs (Small and Medium Enterprises) and microbusinesses more generally.

This means a new organizational and communications model that uses social networking (see WBMI's page on LinkedIn). The new model will organize a constant stream of events, such as the Day of Women's Entrepreneurship, lunches with successful entrepreneurs (such as those organized at Stanford), publications, forums and blogs, television programs (see above), training days, and so on—all under the brand Le Cercle des Entrepreneures.

――――――――――

INTERVIEW WITH EMILIE CREUZIEUX, FOUNDER OF MONBENTO (MENTEE)

Mentoring helps me to ask myself the right questions.

Emilie set up Monbento in 2009, a company based in Clermont-Ferrand in France, which specializes in artisanal food containers.

You're only 31 but you've been an entrepreneur for more than five years!

My very first professional experience was as a freelancer. I'd actually been a physiotherapist for four years, but I wanted to set up my own business, and I hit upon the right product at the right time! Monbento was the answer to one of my personal needs: to find something to carry my lunch in. One day, I discovered a Japanese lunch box called *bento*, which was very practical and aesthetically pleasing. Very quickly, I decided to sell my own lunch boxes by creating Monbento with my partner, a product designer, and a friend who was a web specialist. The company developed very quickly. We succeeded in creating a brand and launching ourselves on the international market: Monbento is now present in more than 40 countries, including the whole of Europe, North America, Brazil, and Asia. The product is adapted to each market—the American lunch box for example—brought up to date with a touch of design. We even have a community that follows us on the Internet, where we also share recipes.

Have you had any mentoring?

My partner had set up a company before me, and so I'd already seen the different steps in the launching of a business. Just before we launched Monbento, I went to the information space called Jeunes de Clermont-Ferrand to help me to draw up a business plan. Since then, I haven't had the time to get involved in a network, but as I work with my partner, I've never had the feeling of isolation, because we discuss things a lot. And don't forget that I'm very involved in the operational side of things. I never thought that I might welcome being able to talk about different problems, the strategy of Monbento, etc., with someone who had already been through the same steps. Having said that, at that time, I had not met any particular problems, and no specific step was therefore required. But with hindsight, I now know that it would have been a good thing to do. And that's why, at the beginning of 2014, I joined the network of Femmes Chefs d'Entreprise (FCE), who contacted me after meeting me at a Paris trade fair.

Why did you want a mentor?

There again, it's something that someone suggested to me. I took part in a competition—the Prix Jeunes Entrepreneurs of the future—and was chosen to participate in the G20 of Young Entrepreneurs.[1] There I met one of the WBMI mentors, Annie Combelles, who encouraged me to apply for the mentoring program. It was a good time to do it because of the growth phase the company was in and because of where I was in my role as chief executive.

What were your needs?

Monbento grew very quickly, particularly in terms of staff. We were going through a head office reorganization in Clermont-Ferrand

---

[1] The G20 of Young Entrepreneurs was set up in 2010 with the goal of bringing young entrepreneurs of member countries together during the G20 conference to share and reflect on a range of possible government actions. www .citizen-entrepreneurs.com/g20-yea/.

and creating two subsidiaries abroad: one in the United States and the other in Hong Kong. I wanted this to succeed, wanted to place the right people in the right positions and to sort out all the problems. The choice of mentor was made with these needs in mind. WBMI thought about mentors who could manage the HR question and the issues of international growth, and suggested I meet Jean-Jacques Berard. The mentoring started at the beginning of 2014 and continued throughout the year. We saw each other once a month, but I know he's always ready to work with me between meetings.

How did your first work meeting go?

Simply: we began by a discussion to analyze where Monbento was and where I was as CEO. We identified different issues and decided on the important areas to look at. Straightaway we formed a good relationship, which is essential because the success of mentoring depends on the quality of the mentor/mentee relationship. I trusted Jean-Jacques and felt no obstacle to communication, which might seem astonishing!

What were the key mentoring moments for your professional career?

Mentoring is useful because it allows you to verbalize what you've got in your head. The mentor doesn't give you a solution or say what you have to do, but helps you to clarify the questions about the company's structure so as to find the key issues or identify the right people. On certain topics, I already had quite a clear vision, and that strengthened my self-confidence. To know that other people have been through the same steps also reassured me. In any case, an entrepreneur needs support, needs to be able to discuss with other chief executives, particularly when the entrepreneur isn't part of a network or has nobody in their team of equal stature. But in my view, young entrepreneurs don't think about mentoring straight off. If someone had offered me a mentoring program, I would probably not have done it, even though it's beneficial today and for the future.

What advice would you give to a woman thinking about following mentoring?

It's easy to hook up with a local network of entrepreneurs, and you can find it in your town or region. And even if they don't offer mentoring, it's useful to surround yourself with other chief executives who have already been through the steps, and above all, not to consider it as a waste of time—rather the contrary!

INTERVIEW WITH JEAN-JACQUES BERARD, CO-FOUNDER OF EXECUTIVE INTERIM MANAGEMENT (MENTOR)

Successful mentoring is like rugby: it's a team victory.

Jean-Jacques is co-founder and Senior Executive Advisor at EIM, as well as founder and CEO of CSM Consult and has been a WBMI mentor since the association started in 2010.

Your professional career is full of executive management experiences...

An engineer by training, I started my career at Radiall in Germany, before attending Stanford, where I gained an MBA. I then returned to Paris and joined McKinsey, a major American consultancy firm, and then the management of Merlin Gerin in Grenoble, which subsequently became Schneider Electric. At this time, in the 1980s, I set up my first company developing a new product of small metal hoses for microcomputing. Today, this company is worth a billion euros! After eight years, I decided to join the Pinault Group, and for two years I headed up an industrial subsidiary in Vendee. Pinault sold off its industrial subsidiaries in 1992, and I stayed on for a few months with the new American buyers before moving to EIM (Executive Interim Management), at the end of 1993. In 1995, together with a few colleagues, we took over the company and renamed it Excellence in Management in order to develop a new concept: change management. Today, EIM has 15 offices around the world and is market leader. Finally in 2009, I set up CSM Consult, a firm specializing in personalized consultancy to managers or shareholders to advise them on the critical steps in the growth of a company.

Why did you decide to become a mentor?

I've always done mentoring because at EIM, I supported a number of CEOs as they took over their posts. To be a mentor in WBMI is part of this work. I set up the Stanford Business Club in 1979, and was president several times. Then I asked Martine Liautaud to take over the presidency. When she had the idea of setting up WBMI, I agreed to be one of the mentors as I really want to help young people! I've always been an entrepreneur: even when I set up my first company within Merlin Gerin, it came to me naturally. Of course, I made mistakes, but you learn through talking with others. It's a shame that, in France, entrepreneurship is not valued. In the United States on the contrary, and especially for all of us who went to Stanford, the desire to set up a company is very strong. I received an injection over there, which led to a reaction. Since then, I've looking for a way to encourage entrepreneurship in France because it can improve the country for future generations.

Were you trained in how to be a mentor before starting to do it?

I learned on the job, as it were, through meetings at work. Our WBMI values were created as and when needed, through a sort of natural co-option, and our aim, at present, is to increase the number of mentees. Each mentee is chosen by a panel on the strength of her application, and the mentor/mentee pairs are created by affinity. The mentor must feel at ease with the context in which the mentee works, without necessarily knowing the mentee herself. Then a discussion between two potential mentors and the candidate takes place, and they talk about her business and her reasons for applying for mentoring. We then decide who the mentor will be, and, of course, the mentee can ask for a different person. That's what I mean by natural co-option. So we have a structure, but one that still remains informal.

Since 2000, you've mentored three entrepreneurs.

I had strong professional relationships with them, even friendship. With each mentoring, I think that I made the mentee take another step forward. The first mentee had a business that was working reasonably well, so I directed my mentoring more to her than to her company. After this mentoring, she changed her career as I had helped her to become aware that it was never too late. The second mentee ran a sales training company, Booster Academy — Evelyne Platnic Cohen is a phenomenon, top of her game. The mentoring was a little special because she knew where she wanted to go, and it required a great deal of tact to mentor this very responsive hyperactive mentee who displayed a lot of leadership qualities! I adapted to this mentoring by listening to Evelyne without asking her to do anything, since any decisions had to come from her. I helped her to have a vision and a strategy for her company and to imagine the organization by rising above the operational level. There are two reasons to set up a company: for oneself and for others. The second option assumes ambition and power sharing to be able to grow. Entrepreneurship is not an individual sport, but a collective one. Evelyne is a woman of results, someone who knows how to reach the goal. I currently mentor Emilie Creuzieux. She's also a very ambitious leader, blessed with extraordinary drive and great potential. Mentoring her is not straightforward because she is very down to earth and acts quickly. We have a relationship of great trust. I guide her in strategy, and give her theoretical grounding in management and how to run a company, in order to give her reference points. She is keen to learn, intuitive, and understands very quickly. She loves a challenge, fears nothing and moves ahead quickly. I admire her a lot! I see no limits to her progress ... sometimes I'd like to be in her place!

What have been the key moments in these experiences?

I'm proud of having put my first mentee back on track as a person, and of helping the second to adopt a more communal approach by finding organizational links and helping her to develop a network of franchises. Finally, I am proud that my third mentee has responded so well to my advice. A company is three things: the product, the people, and the process—what I call the 3Ps; over it all is strategy. In Emilie's company, there are too many products, not enough people and no processes. She understood this very quickly and correcting it became her priority. She started to aim for performance with more cohesion in her staff in order to produce profitable growth.

Have there been any difficulties?

You can't come to mentoring with a method worked out in advance. Mentoring is not for beginners. You have to find the right method for each person and each company. The mentor sees what he can bring to the relationship depending on his own experience. Mentoring is a really customized activity.

What have you gained from these experiences?

I've had an excellent experience because it's a pleasure to see others succeed and to do something. I thought I knew women, but in reality I didn't know them well enough professionally. The women I've mentored are professional and, when convinced, are results oriented, without doubt more than men on average. On the other hand, they have difficulty conceptualizing or having a long-term vision. That makes me to think about how to get the most out of the male/female mentoring relationship—from a managerial perspective—so that it could become a new way to improve the company performance.

INTERVIEW WITH MURIELE ROOS, FOUNDER OF FEMME MAJUSCULE (MENTEE)

My mentor gives me the energy I need to continue.

Muriele set up and runs a bimonthly magazine called *Femme Majuscule*, which is aimed at women aged 45 and over.

Before going into the magazine world, you had a brilliant career in marketing...

After ESSEC, I joined Danone in 1987 as Assistant Product Manager for Kronenbourg. I first worked in Greece for a beer brand that the group had taken over, and then became head of the group at Evian where I piloted the relaunch of the brand. Later, in 1995, I was appointed director of the Heudebert brand, where I led the negotiation campaigns with two buying groups, before taking over as head of Marketing and Development at Volvic, and then of the whole group that was formed out of Volvic's merger with Evian. I left Danone for Well in 1998. I was beginning to think increasingly about the place of women in society and I wanted to do something. At the start of my forties, when I had just had my second child, I made my decision and set up my company "50 etc." I wanted to offer a box of samples to women over 50, similar to the box of samples that new mothers receive on the birth of their child, but within the context of breast cancer screening. The regional test worked well, but I couldn't persuade the brands to do a national launch. That spurred me to directly address women, and in 2011 I created *Femme Majuscule* aimed at women aged 45 to 50 and older. I started from the fact that, by the end of 2014, 50 percent of women in France would be aged around 50 or older. In creating this magazine I was going against the tide, which is thrilling but hard work—a little like attacking a mountain with a teaspoon. When you read *Femme Majuscule*, you find women who look like you—they're all at least 40 years old, including the models. The aim is to motivate women to keep going and not get demoralized by the pervading images of youth that surround us. With *Femme Majuscule*, I feel I'm participating in a change in our society. I feel a great satisfaction when readers write and say they feel "capital women" and thank us for what we've done for them!

Before turning to a mentor, had you been supported in any way before?

Not to speak of, apart from having a coach when I was on the steering committee of Well. He coached me through a difficult patch; when you're at the head of a company, you can be assailed by doubts, but you can't always speak to the members of your team or to friends, since neither are really there for that reason. I am sometimes overwhelmed by crises, and I lose my vision for the company; then in 2011 Dominique Maire, a friend and mentor at WBMI, told me about the association, which had just been founded. But I didn't take the plunge. Then one day it became clear—what was I waiting

for? Perhaps I was afraid of disturbing people or of not being interesting enough? But now I know that Dominique was right to speak
to me about it.

What did you need to get out of mentoring?

My husband, who is a CEO, helped me, financially, to launch the
project. But after three years he asked me to become financially
independent, which is fair enough. This was like an electric
shock—but it did me good. I had to ask myself if I'd made the
right choices, if my business model was sound, how I could raise
funds. I needed to be a bit more objective, to find a new vision and
to be reassured, above all in the face of bad advisors ... so I joined
WBMI, and they helped me to find the right path; Eve Magnant
became my mentor in May 2013.

What did you learn from her?

She's my Jiminy Cricket! I'm always happy to see her, she's like a
breath of fresh air that inspires me! Eve keeps an experienced eye
on me. She gives me the energy I need to keep going. Sometimes,
when I'm at the end of my tether, I call her, and she reassures me by
pointing out how far I've come, and other things that I may have
lost sight of. She also knows how to push me, ever so nicely, by
reminding me that I haven't done such and such that I said I'd do.
She also makes me get out of my little bubble and tell the world
what I'm doing. I feel very free with her these days. We see each
other every 10 or 15 days, and I contact her whenever I need to. She
gives me back my self-confidence and reminds me that what I do is
valuable and important for women—and for advertisers, who are
not always easy to persuade! You see, those first three really busy
years at the start made me lose sight of the value—mine as well
as the project's—especially in the fast-changing magazine sector.
But more than simply a magazine, *Femme Majuscule* is a partner
to women; and therefore I need the means to scale it up. My mentor has opened doors for me, made me meet people. A virtuous
circle has been started. And because of that, I'm beginning to see

how digital could help me. Internet is a real challenge for *Femme Majuscule* and may be able to deliver services I wanted to deliver at the start. Overall, I feel a lot more comfortable about where I'm going!

What were the key moments in your professional life?

For example, for the March 2014 anniversary edition, I had a lot of reviews in the media (radio, press, etc.), and this success is closely linked to Eve and WBMI. Their care and lack of any vested interest are crucial. I feel that my mentor, together with all the WBMI team, want to put entrepreneurs into the limelight so that they take their rightful place in the economy. I've become aware that sometimes you just have to go for it, even if you're not completely ready, because it's better to throw yourself into something than to miss the boat.

What has this experience brought you?

I hope that it's not over yet! There's still a way to go. In 2013, I said that I'd never manage it, I was ready to call it a day. This feeling has now gone, and I know I'll find a way forward. Today the magazine is better known, and our subscriptions are on the increase. I feel reassured, even if the adventure is still complex. And I have beliefs that I'm happy to tell the world; I feel more armed and more certain about things. Many women can't speak for themselves, so I tell myself that through *Femme Majuscule* I can be someone who speaks for them. If you really want to change the world, you can't accept all the male values! Diversity has benefits for both men and women, in their lives as well as in their work. And you have to remember that generations live together with values, with desires, with different projects.... Mentoring helps to bridge these gaps, because there's no vested interest, unlike coaching, which is based on a financial contract, although it has its place. In any case, if I succeed with my project, I dream of becoming a mentor in my turn, to pass on what I have learned to the next generation—especially the next generation! I now feel a responsibility to help others.

_____

INTERVIEW WITH EVE MAGNANT, VP AT PUBLICIS (MENTOR)

The mentor is certainly not a passive spectator!

Eve is Vice President and Director of Corporate Social Responsibility at the Publicis Groupe.

What is your professional career to date?

I did a degree in sociology in Paris, then I did two master's, one in political sciences and the other in communications. As I was coming up to my forties, I did an Executive MBA at HEC. In terms of work, after three years in a small communications agency I joined Publicis where I've been for 23 years now. At Publicis, I've done three jobs. The first was operational, I was Corporate and Crisis Communications Advisor to major groups for 12 years; then I took a functional role as director of the Group's Corporate Communications. Since 2007, I've been director of the Group's Corporate Social Responsibility.

Did you want to be a mentor, or did someone suggest it to you?

I wanted to do it because I've been mentoring different groups for 10 years or so already: young graduates with diverse backgrounds, women from the European Professional Women's Network (EPWN), and Publicis employees. I am also a member of several networks such as EPWN, HEC, HEC/AFIP (an association aimed at supporting professional integration), and WCD (Women Corporate Directors) among others; in addition, I started up an internal network of women working in Publicis Groupe some years ago, called VivaWomen!, driving several activities to support our women in their career path, including a mentoring program.

What motivated you to become a mentor?

Within WBMI, we have always worked, together with Martine Liautaud, from the fact that women entrepreneurs, already fewer in number that men, are in even more need of support than men and should not find themselves alone. Yet it is difficult to find support, which is free of charge, caring, and with no vested interest. As a company manager, I know how important it is to have someone with whom you can speak freely, without constraints, on a range of subjects, and sometimes to receive advice. Our only aim is to help our mentees to achieve their goals. Before agreeing to be a mentor at WBMI, I was made aware of my role in order to clarify what a mentor is, and what it is not.

How was your mentee chosen?

WBMI's selection panel chose *Femme Majuscule*, a bimonthly magazine for women, on objective criteria: it was a company more than three years old, founded by a woman, with important development issues. We also knew how daring the project was in that it was a woman founder of a magazine aimed at women between 45 and 50 years old. It's not only relevant (in terms of the demographic) but also quite bold because the press is going through a difficult period in France at the moment.... As it was media, my profession made me Muriele Roos's natural mentor. It's important to remember that WBMI is also an internal network: there are 12 mentors with different professional backgrounds and different areas of expertise. One of us is the main mentor and closest to the mentee, and the other mentors are resources to whom we can turn whenever there is a specific need. This extended support is very important and is our distinguishing feature.

How was the first meeting with Muriele?

We started with a very long meeting in the editorial offices of *Femme Majuscule* in the eighteenth district of Paris; we looked at all the issues, the questions, the priorities ... and we got to know each other. Mentoring is first and foremost about the meetings. Our meetings need to be effective and pleasant, and without constraints! This experience, which is still underway, is supposed to last a year, but you have to be aware of the nature of the issues, which sometimes take longer to deal with.

What are the highlights of this experience?

Each new issue of *Femme Majuscule* is a source of joy, and it's very infectious! Muriele has moments of intense satisfaction, and rightly so: when she talks to her readers at a trade fair, for example, she gets the impression that her magazine is responding to an expectation... or when *Femme Majuscule* writes about something quite daring, different from what you might read elsewhere, and the mail to the magazine is full of thanks. And she's had a number of productive meetings, which have helped her directly and indirectly.

Have there been any difficulties?

There are moments of discouragement, which are quite understandable because Muriele is alone when facing difficulties. Even though she has a small but effective team, she is the decision maker and the person responsible; she has to make 100 decisions a day, from the simplest (buying light bulbs) to the more difficult: an advertiser decides to shift his advertising campaign at the last minute, and it affects more than a fourth of the coverage at the deadline! Happily, she finds a solution. My job is to support her at each of these times and to understand each situation and Muriele's state of mind, and to help her to find a way to move forward in the right direction... this is not always easy because an entrepreneur's life is like doing the hurdles. So the mentor is certainly not a passive spectator! Even though it's the mentor who guides the entrepreneur in how to jump the hurdles, it's nevertheless the entrepreneur herself who has to jump them.

What has this experience brought you?

It might seem trite to say that it's brought me great richness at a human level, but it's true. The meetings we had gave me the opportunity to think about new subjects but also to make me question my usefulness and my role. And nothing is prescribed: we have had to create the path for *Femme Majuscule*. Every path seems wide and long before you take it, but the access route is steep! For my part, I want to continue as a mentor, as each project is unique and interesting. As an employee, I admire entrepreneurs like Muriele a lot, her vision and her tenacity, and her project seems to me to be just right.

INTERVIEW WITH JANE CHEN, CO-FOUNDER OF EMBRACE

> I've always believed that when you find your calling, the universe conspires to help you achieve it.

Jane is the co-founder and CEO of Embrace, a social enterprise that aims to help millions of vulnerable babies born every year in developing countries through a low-cost infant warmer: the Thermpod. The Thermpod looks like a miniature sleeping bag and provides a lifesaving four to six hours of heat. Unlike traditional incubators that cost up to $20,000, it costs around $200, requires no electricity, has no moving parts, is portable and is safe and intuitive to use.

While Jane was pursuing her MBA at Stanford in 2008, she enrolled in a multidisciplinary class: Entrepreneurial Design for Extreme Affordability. In that class, she teamed up with graduate students in computer science, electrical engineering, and material science and developed the Thermpod. The team raised funding from Echoing Green, a New York City–based outfit that makes grants to social entrepreneurs, and the family-oriented David & Lucile Packard Foundation. After a successful pilot program in India, Embrace struck a global distribution deal with GE Healthcare.

How did you decide to become an entrepreneur?

I got into this after college and after doing management consulting for a few years; one day I read an article in the *New York Times* about the AIDS epidemic in China; basically all the blood they collected was pooled together and separated, and the red blood cells were re-injected back into everyone's bodies, and as a result, 60 to 80 percent of the adult population was HIV positive. When I read the article, a light bulb in my head went off, and I realized we were some of the luckiest people in the world, and I could have easily been born into a different life where I could have contracted this fatal disease. At that point, I felt very strongly about it so I quit my job and, over the next two years helped out students—we sponsored their education fees, but more importantly, the Chinese government stepped up, providing re-education and free medication for everyone that was testing positive. And I met a group of people who were dedicated and passionate and able to effect social change in a big way. But from my experience, and through my experience with an equipment foundation in Tanzania, I saw many people lose their lives because they weren't able to adapt medicine or technology, and it was really frustrating to see that. And so I decided it would be my personal mission to try to bridge this huge disparity that I saw in health care and, in effect, to try to democratize health care for the poor people of the world.

So Embrace started while I was at business school. The program brought together people from different masters programs, and we were asked to work on a technology project that would help people who had to live on a dollar a day. And the challenge at the time, for my team, was to build a baby incubator that cost 1 percent of the cost a traditional incubator cost, which was about $20,000. So we travelled to Nepal, and India, and we discovered that one of the biggest problems they face is that the incubators require a constant supply of electricity and they're very difficult to operate and require many things that you don't find in rural areas. So we developed an incubator with wax in the lining that uses hot water or a short burst of electricity to heat the wax, and it heats up to the right temperature, which is retained for eight hours.

The product is great—but how did you go from developing the product as a business school project to actually creating the company?

I've always believed that when you find your calling, the universe conspires to help you achieve it. And that has happened again and again in my own life—and so along the way, I found incredible resources. I didn't require any job since I was in my second year of business school; and with my team we entered every business competition to get the money, and we actually did not win most of them, but a few days before I graduated, we won two competitions on the same day. That gave us the money to start, and the rest was just figuring it out along the way. We had the strategy in place, and we had the team, and we were really open minded about how things would go, and we had an idea of where our destination would be, but the way you're going to get there is going to vary—and you have to be very opportunistic in your approach to how to get to your destination. So we faced, of course, many barriers along the way—it was, you know, it was grueling—I remember India (after we graduated I lived in India for the next four years), and it was the hardest thing I've ever done in my life. Starting a business in India is—there's good and bad but you can't imagine how difficult it is in terms of bureaucracy—nothing goes the way it's supposed to there, it's incredibly frustrating, but a couple of things helped me. One was having the support of an amazing group of people—I had advisors along the way—advisors in India, advisors in the United States and in Stanford with a bunch of really powerful alumni—people that were connected in India. And those people were so incredibly helpful in introducing us to the right people, getting things off the ground. I've had personal mentors along the way. And then I think the other thing that was really important as an entrepreneur is to be relating your purpose. I think that when you're doing something that means so much to you, it's very helpful, because when things get really hard, and there are many moments when you want to quit, you just ask yourself if this is worth it. And for me, when I go back through the stories and the babies we helped, and the mothers we helped, when things are hard, I reflect on the people and the moments and why I am doing all of this, and that gives me the strength to keep going.

In those moments of despair, is it your own reflections, or are there people who helped you through?

Yes, there's no way that I could have done what I did alone. There were many people along the way and to be honest, some of them were excited enough to join us; many people left their jobs in the United States, people who were so talented: my co-founders, people who joined us for six months or a year, some of the brightest people I've ever had the chance to work with—joining a cause—and that gives you a tremendous amount of energy.

They all had remarkable backgrounds: I'd often look around the room and think, *if we can't solve this problem, then I don't know who can!*

So yes, absolutely, mentorship, but I think you have to have that inner compass as well, you know, that true north. In India, there were always people around, but I think having that moral compass and being able to remind yourself why you were so convinced to do something in the first place. You know, sometimes I think you lose sight of that, and you get caught up in the leaves trying to make numbers or payroll, and you can decide it's not worth it—unless you believe in that inner compass.

What advice would you give to other women entrepreneurs when they meet obstacles?

Well, as I said earlier, there are a couple of things; think about why you're doing what you're doing. The other thing is that, as a CEO, you might think, *I should be this, I should be that, I should be top*—but after a while I realized that the best CEOs, the best leaders, are the ones that find their own way, their own style. You know, the work I do is inherently emotional, so exhibit your emotions. You know, one time, I can't remember exactly what it was, I was really troubled by something, and I cried in front of my team, and I was mortified—it was the first time I'd ever cried in front of my team, and you know what, one of my team, my COO, came up to me afterwards and he thanked me and he said, "Thank you so much for doing that, because when you show your vulnerability, other people can as well." Showing your vulnerability, showing people who you are—that allows people to connect with you and believe in you as a leader.

And the other thing I'd say is focus on your own happiness. For a long time, I thought that if I could just get Embrace in place, then I could focus on my own happiness in my personal life. Then I read this wonderful article about managers and leaders who are happy, their teams perform so much better because the happiness of a leader is contagious, kind of powerful—and I realized that if I'm happy, and have that balance, then that makes them much better leaders.

INTERVIEW WITH ABIGAIL HOLSBOROUGH, FOUNDER OF ROUTEMAP

As an entrepreneur, mentoring is the best help you can get.

Abigail is an entrepreneur and founder of the start-up, RouteMap, which provides alternative access evidence for young people trying to choose what to do beyond school—entering university or the workplace—via internships, apprenticeships, or directly into jobs.

Can you tell me briefly about your business career?

I've only recently left university, on a sort of self-directed gap year. I basically learnt to code with an organization called Code First: Girls,[2] sponsored by the City of London and Royal Bank of Scotland. It aims to give girls an introduction to coding and the tech world in general—what the tech ecosystem is and how can you get into it. That was in the summer of 2013, and ever since then I've been hooked. I started to learn to code and do weekly coding practice, and then I had this idea for RouteMap—but had no way of creating it at that time. So I went back to university and started to look for funding opportunities—different grants and accelerator programs. I pitched my idea to my mentor at the time, and he loved it, and he was more than happy to come on board with me. So when I left university again, in April last year, we officially started RouteMap and by December had been accepted into the Wayra UnLtd Accelerator, backed by Telefonica.[3]

Do you feel there are any obstacles to women setting up businesses—or even just working—in the tech industry?

My background was not technical. I did economics and had originally planned to do Chinese studies—tech wasn't my thing. The tech industry is often pitched as a boys' world—the common

---

[2]www.codefirstgirls.org.uk/.
[3]https://unltd.org.uk/path/wayra-unltd/ and http://wayra.co.

perception of the start-up world is computer geek boys eating pizza and drinking beer, which can be off-putting for females who don't feel they belong in that scene. I think the biggest obstacle to women (and men) setting up businesses in this industry is how much people mythicize the stories of successful entrepreneurs. Men like Jobs and Zuckerberg are put on these unreachable pedestals, where their successes are the only part of their stories that people focus on, and that can add undue pressure to founders to be perfect from the start. I still find it hard to accept the fact that I will inevitably make mistakes, and, as an entrepreneur, it's hard to keep yourself motivated to keep asking for help.

People often say that women undersell themselves, and I think in business I do that quite a bit. I think it can be very hard because, as soon as you start up a business, it's constant pitching. Whether you even realize it or not, you're constantly trying to sell yourself, your story, your team, your idea. And you have to be—sometimes as a woman in front of an all-male panel—very sure of yourself and your abilities—very sure of your ability to lead a team and to turn this idea into something that can be profitable and viable. I felt I had to be better than the guys, because there are some men that you meet, who can be quite dismissive of women when they come up against you in competitions or accelerators. If you internalize that, it will make you worry that you're not good enough to be there, or, as I said, you default into underselling yourself and your skills.

So what's the way around that?

The way around that—first and foremost, everyone says it changes with time—experience shows you that you are good enough to be here and you grow more confident. But before you get all that experience, you need people who have had that experience to reassure you and remind you that you should be confident in yourself. I guess that's where a mentor comes into the equation.

Governments and corporations across the globe are trying to encourage girls into STEM (science, technology, engineering, and math) and coding in separate programs like the one I completed. These do have an impact, but I think the best way to help women feel more able to participate is to highlight the stories of other female engineers and entrepreneurs. Hearing about successful women, both the struggles and breakthroughs in their careers, can be one of the best inspirations.

Have you had any mentoring yourself?

I've had a lot of mentoring—not only through formal programs that I've applied to but also informally networking with people that I've met—in banking, when I interned at UBS, Deutsche Bank and Barclays, as well as programs supporting young people to apply to Cambridge. We recently got into the top 20 for a competition called iDEA (Inspiring Digital Enterprise Award) backed by HRH The Duke of York,[4] which aims to help young people set up tech businesses. So yesterday in fact I met my mentor—I was very nervous about meeting him—but we have a weekly breakfast meeting, so that we can develop my pitch and prepare for the finals. Before our first meeting, I mapped out the different components of our business model, as well as the assumptions we've made about our target market and tried to identify our weak points. We went through it together and used it to make a plan of how we'll get through each of those areas over the next six weeks that we'll work together. This mentoring mainly focuses on my business needs.

On a more personal level, I have an informal mentor whom I met before I applied to the accelerator program. I literally Googled everybody and anybody who was connected to the UnLtd where I won my first business grant, and I found a woman called Natalie Campbell,[5] who runs a company called A Very Good Company, and I literally sent her a tweet saying, "Hello. You do X, Y, Z.

---

[4]The Duke of York and Nominet Trust initiative iDEA: Digital Enterprise Award Scheme, to encourage young people to start their own business ventures. https://www.onemillionyoungideas.org.uk/.
[5]Natalie is a founding partner at A Very Good Company and also Trustee of UnLtd, The Foundation for Social Entrepreneurs, as well as a board member of Wayra UnLtd, a "tech for good" accelerator program funded by O2 Telefonica and the Cabinet Office. http://cloresocialleadership.org.uk/natalie_campbell.

Will you have a coffee with me?" And she agreed. She's just been amazing. I think a week before we did the final pitch to get into this accelerator program, I emailed her, and I was like, "I don't know what I'm doing; I'm so nervous my pitch doesn't sound good enough, it's not a minute long or whatever it had to be." And she said "Okay. Stop. Come and meet me, and let's talk through it." And she gave me practical advice on the pitch; she is just a very reassuring person — again it's saying small things like "Don't worry. You'll be fine. You know you can do this. You've done X, Y, Z." Helping to remind you of your past successes and therefore bolstering your self-confidence.

How would you assess mentoring?

As an entrepreneur, mentoring is the best help you can get. I'm a big fan of Tai Lopez, who argues that even if you can't find access to a mentor, some of the world's greatest minds are instantly accessible to us through books and videos, and that still counts as a form of mentoring. For me, especially being as young as I am, mentors effectively are wise sounding boards I can turn to for decision making or just to know that I'm on the right track. Eventually, some of these relationships have become more formalized as people opt to become advisors for the business, and the expertise and networks they bring to the table are a big help.

What advice would you give to other women entrepreneurs?

Whenever you go into business, you're always told to look for people in your industry or field that you admire. The whole point of that is to learn from them. If you're able to get a mentoring relationship, whether formal or informal, it's the perfect opportunity to learn from somebody, because they can help you avoid some of the big pitfalls that they've had and also share the ways that they've found success, different approaches they've taken, lessons that they've learned — they can pass that all on to you, and you're able to benefit from their experience. But also, they're sharing your journey with you as you continue. They're people to celebrate with and people to share your disappointments with and people to help you wake up the next day and continue. I think everybody talks about the glamorous side of business, but they don't know how hard it can be sometimes, how isolating it can be—even if you have a business partner, because it gets hard and you need people who can just pep you up. A mentor is never meant to be perfect, just another human who you feel that you can learn something from. Be bold in reaching out to people, share your story, and in time try and pass on the lessons you've learned to someone else.

What advice might you give a girl going into the tech industry?

The best piece of advice I was given was to not pressure yourself to know everything straightaway. With tech, there are so many things to learn, and there always will be because of updates in technology. I think girls, if you feel like you have a point to prove, you want to show the boys that you know everything and you can do this and do that, and be independent and build or code or do things for yourself, you have to remember that it's no fault to your character if you don't know things—as long as you show a willingness to learn. And again, it's to your mentors that you show that willingness, because they're able to teach you the skills or point you in the right direction for information. Don't be scared of the boys, I'd say, because some people talk themselves up a bit, and everybody was a beginner, boy or girl, at some time. As long as you know where you stand, skill-wise, confidence-wise, etc., you say, *This is the point that I'm at; and these are the targets I'm aiming for; and these are the skills I need to build to get there.* And you just need to find ways to do that.

INTERVIEW WITH CLARA SHIH, FOUNDER OF HEARSAY SOCIAL

I've been mentored my whole life, and it's made an incredible difference.

Clara is the CEO and founder of Hearsay Social, which uses predictive analytics technology to help salespeople contact clients at the right time and with the right message. Clara developed the first social business application in 2007, and was named one of *Fortune* magazine's Most Powerful Women Entrepreneurs, *BusinessWeek's* Top Young Entrepreneurs, both *Fortune's* and *Ad Age's* 40 under 40, and Young Global Leader by the World Economic Forum.

Clara is a member of the Starbucks board of directors and previously served in a range of technical, product, and marketing roles at Google, Microsoft, and Salesforce.com. She graduated in Computer Science at Stanford University and also holds an MS in Internet Studies from Oxford University.

Tell me about your career and how you became entrepreneur.

I first thought about becoming an entrepreneur after Stanford, where I knew my co-founder, and where there was a highly entrepreneurial environment. We were both engineering students, and we were surrounded by, and influenced by, a lot of role models—we caught the excitement that was going on around us. We actually didn't decide to become entrepreneurs right away, although we did talk about it during the time we were at school. After graduating, I worked at Microsoft, Google, and Salesforce before starting Hearsay Social.

I got quite comfortable working at a big company, but I always had a lingering question in the back of my mind. The catalyst for me to start the company was that I happened to be at the first Facebook hackathon, and I ended up building an app that went viral. The app was written about in the tech press as being the first business app on Facebook. When news of the app got out, several publishers contacted me, and it resulted in me writing one of the first books about how to use Facebook for sales and marketing, which convinced me that social business was a real opportunity and was going to be huge. With the book coming out, I decided to quit my job at Salesforce, and called up my old friend from Stanford, and the two of us started Hearsay Social in my living room.

Do you see any obstacles preventing women from choosing entrepreneurship as a career or preventing them from scaling up?

I'd say that there are three major obstacles. Number one is that there is a pipeline problem. Whether you're a man or a woman, you're likely to feel most confident and be successful starting a tech company if you have a technical background. If you look at the numbers of women pursuing STEM degrees in the universities and graduate schools, it pales in comparison with the number of men. So the pool of people who typically have the set of qualifications that tech investors look for, and where you can start a company without relying on anyone else because you can do all the coding yourself, is just smaller for women. That's one.

Number two is—maybe it affects both men and women—but perhaps women who decide to start families and are not in a 50/50 partnership with their significant other might opt out of starting a company because it's all-consuming. If they don't have that support at home, or they don't feel confident, they opt out. Hence Sheryl Sandberg's book *Lean In*.

And the third obstacle is a systemic issue with women having to overcome perceptions and conscious or unconscious bias from investors, partners, or early employers.

What can we do to support women to overcome these obstacles?

With the first obstacle, I think there's more we can do to reach women earlier on in the educational career to encourage them, to provide role models, and hopefully keep them in the STEM field for longer.

With the second obstacle, opting out, I think the role of mentors, sponsors, and role models is important to encourage women to lean in and take risks and even be aware that this is a career option for them.

And the third obstacle, in terms of the endemic bias: venture capital, for example, is a world of men, and while we have to start working on their unconscious bias, we also need to get venture capital more diverse as a whole. I believe that the more women venture capitalists there are, the more women will get funded.

What about mentoring—is it useful to help women overcome the obstacles?

I've been mentored my whole life, and it's made an incredible difference. At Hearsay Social, which is very much a start-up, we don't have a formal mentoring program, but we have informal mentoring, and, in addition to mentoring, I think sponsors and role models are also an important part of the formula.

21

Networking

IN THE UNITED STATES, WOMEN ENTREPRENEURS find support from a variety of different sources, but one in particular is professional networks.

Two programs illustrate the use of professional networks: Dell's DWEN, and Astia's Community of Experts.

Astia, a California company founded in 1999 in Silicon Valley as a nonprofit organization, has set up a Community of Experts committed to supporting women as entrepreneurs and leaders in high-growth businesses, fueling innovation and driving economic growth. Astia now raises funds to support women entrepreneurs.

DELL WOMEN'S ENTREPRENEUR NETWORK

Through the Dell Women's Entrepreneur Network (DWEN), Dell connects women entrepreneurs across the globe with networks, sources of capital, knowledge, and technology, giving them the power to do more.

DWEN unites top global women owners in an entrepreneurial community. By spotlighting women's entrepreneurial success and creating a supportive atmosphere, DWEN helps a group of like-minded women share best practices, build business opportunities through collaboration, explore international expansion, and access new resources that support business growth.

DWEN hosts an annual Network Event, which is an invitation-only gathering of women founders, CEOs, and thought leaders. They come together to discuss their most pressing business issues and consider how technology can help ignite growth in today's increasingly global economy. In 2013, DWEN launched an initiative (Pay It Forward) to mobilize successful business owners and leaders to help more than one million aspiring women entrepreneurs by the end of 2015.

DWEN is more than an annual event; it's a community of women entrepreneurs from over 11 countries collaborating to grow their businesses and connecting through social platforms including LinkedIn, Twitter, Flickr, and Storify. In between the annual events, intimate networking events are hosted by Dell and attended by women business owners in major cities around the world.[1]

INTERVIEW WITH STÉPHANIE CARDOT, FOUNDER AND CEO OF TO DO TODAY

In such programs as DWEN, one needs to be both on the receiving and the giving back end.

Created in September 2001, TO DO TODAY was the first company in France to provide on-site Corporate Concierge and Well-Being services, designed to improve employee morale and engagement, as well as attraction and retention of talents. With a wide range of services, from on-site beautician, barber, hairdresser, dry cleaning, shoe repairs, errand running, TO DO TODAY has grown into other European countries and is now establishing a presence in the United States.

Could you tell us about your professional career? How did you decide to become an entrepreneur?

I started my career in the United States at Deloitte, first as Manager of Community Relations, then as Manager of International Business Development.

---

[1] Source: www.dell.com/learn/us/en/uscorp1/women-powering-business.

There I learned two things:

1. A service provider is first and foremost a *solution* provider (i.e., being creative and innovative, but within the client's corporate culture and financial constraints).
2. It's not about the idea, it's about how you *deliver* it (i.e., being process-oriented).

After five years, I returned to France and met an entrepreneur with a great concept, who suggested we started a business together, which I did enthusiastically, investing all my savings in the process. It turned out to be an amazing experience, especially after my partner ran away with the money, and I had to file for bankruptcy in three different countries and spend a whole year closing down the business.

By then, I was fully ready for entrepreneurship and launched TO DO TODAY, which has had two-figure growth every year, for the past 14 years.

In what program do you participate?

Among others, I have been a member of DWEN (Dell's Women Entrepreneur Network) since 2012. Every year, Dell invites DWEN members to a two-to-three-day program in a different location. The agenda is a mix between experience sharing, listening to visionary entrepreneurs who share their recipes for success (and warnings about failures), hearing about how technology can help us bring our businesses to the next level. Most importantly, it allows for strong international networking and business opportunities for those of us looking to expand internationally.

Every year, we pick up the conversation right where we left it the year before, and most of us continue sharing ideas in between events.

How did you hear about that program and why did you decide to participate? What were your needs?

I was approached by the DWEN team, which was looking to invite their first group of French entrepreneurs into the program.

I embraced this program for two main reasons:

1. I had been an entrepreneur in France for 11 years, was losing myself in administrative and regulatory hassles, and had lost some of my energy. Reconnecting with female entrepreneurs from around the globe gave me the "*second souffle*" (second breath) I needed to reboot my ambition and my vision.

2. DWEN is as much a collective mentoring program as an individual one, although each of us knows that we can reach out to our Dell business advisors and friends anytime if we need individual support.

Had you previously considered mentoring schemes?

I've always had mentors, but never in a formalized manner. My parents, both entrepreneurs and exceptionally caring parents, have been my first mentors in life and continue to be, every step of the way. In addition, every work experience allows for informal mentoring, whether with a boss, a more experienced team member, a long-standing client....

Entrepreneurship is about making decisions every single minute, some you're certain of, some you're not. And you can't just follow your guts every time.... It's far more efficient to get advice from more experienced people than trying to reinvent the wheel every day.

How did your first meeting go? What did this experience bring you?

My first DWEN event was a real turning point for me: I was reminded that the sky is the limit! I revisited my growth strategy, assessed my skill set, and decided to focus on international development rather than remaining confined to a single market, however successful I was.

I heard some inspiring stories and decided it was high time to come out of my comfort zone and put myself at risk again.

The DWEN network really came through for me: Whether through IT or business advice, networking opportunities...

everyone at Dell is available to help and support our new ventures.

Were there any difficulties?

No difficulty whatsoever. But also because I am very open to advice and constructive criticism. I have no problem admitting what my weaknesses are, and that makes for an even greater opportunity.

What advice would you give to a woman thinking about participating in the DWEN program?

In such programs as DWEN, one needs to be both on the receiving and the giving back end.

My commitment to the program includes helping and mentoring younger female entrepreneurs to the best of my abilities.

What qualities should a mentor and mentee have?

A mentor needs to be both benevolent and extremely demanding. Any mentoring process requires assessments at set dates to evaluate results within a given timeframe: the mentee needs to be committed to this process, hence recognizing the mentor's own commitment and efforts.

ASTIA: A DIFFERENT KIND OF NETWORK PERFORMING IN A DIFFERENT KIND OF WAY

Astia was founded in Silicon Valley in 1999 as a nonprofit organization dedicated to identifying and promoting best-in-class women high-growth entrepreneurs.[2]

Today, Astia operates globally with nodes in San Francisco, New York, and London.

---

[2]This presentation is an extract from the White Paper "Astia—Investing in the Success of Women High Growth Entrepreneurs, Their Teams and Their Ventures" by Teresa Neson and Sharon Vosmek ©2014. For more information, see also www.astia.org.

Since its creation, Astia chose the companies and entrepreneurs to support. Concurrently Astia built a powerful network of more than 5,000 men and women around the world who shared its vision of female-male top teams as an investment strategy.

Astia's expert network is made of highly dedicated individuals who serve as reviewers, evaluators, and advisors. It includes serial entrepreneurs, angel investors, venture capitalists, corporate leaders, bankers, accountants, and lawyers, who donate thousands of professional hours annually.

The Astia Six-Step Company Engagement Process

Astia follows a six-step process (Expert Sift™ Process) as it identifies, evaluates, and partners with high-growth companies and their entrepreneurs and leaders

1. **Personalized Referral**

   Astia advisors around the globe have their eyes open for high-potential start-ups with inclusive founding teams.

2. **Criteria Screen**

   Applicants must meet Astia's criteria. Astia considers visionary companies at any growth stage beyond concept-only, within the sectors of high tech, life sciences, clean tech, consumer tech, and high-growth consumer products and services. At a minimum, start-ups must have at least one woman in a position of influence and equity.

3. **Industry Screen**

   Experts with 15-plus years of industry experience review company materials and provide insight and feedback on the market opportunity.

4. **Operations Screen**

   Corporate executives and serial venture-backed entrepreneurs screen applicants, providing critical operational and management feedback.

5. **Investor Screen**

   Accredited investors, including Astia Angels, attend regular in-person presentations of applicant companies in San Francisco, New York, and London. Astia gathers feedback from investors.

6. **Astia Executive Team Screen**

Includes verification and update of company-provided detail, identification of community acceleration opportunities, review for potential conflicts of interest, advisee company mix, as well as analysis of potential intercompany synergies.

Astia Global Venture Lunches

Entrepreneurs meeting the Astia entrepreneur criteria have the opportunity to present at Astia Global Venture Lunches delivered monthly in San Francisco, New York, and London. Global Venture Lunches bring Astia Angels together with a contingent of nonaffiliated investors to give entrepreneurs wide access to expertise and investment.

Astia Angels

Launched in 2013, Astia Angels is a program under the Astia nonprofit legal umbrella. Astia Angels is a global network of accredited investors made up of women and men who individually consider and make investments in the Astia-qualified companies that are making their way through the Expert Sift™ Process.

The inter-relationship of the Astia nonprofit organization creates value. Astia executive staff directs entrepreneurs to the expertise, resources, capital, and development they need while the entrepreneurs prepare and pitch to Astia Angels for early-stage and follow-on equity capital. Feedback loops provide Astia staff with company referrals from Astia Advisors as well as refinement recommendations on the system itself. Companies move along the pipeline when they are ready to move.

Astia Impact (2003–2014)

VOLUNTEER EXPERTS

5,000 → Number of experts in the volunteer network

450 → Number of corporate executives in the network

950 → Number of experts actively advising Astia companies in 2014

ENTREPRENEUR FIRMS

4,900 → Number of companies reviewed

1,960 → Number of companies enrolled in Astia training

810 → Number of companies presented to investment community

30 → Successful exits; 3 IPOs

THE ENGAGED PUBLIC

>2 million → Number of people touched with the Astia Message

21,000 → Number of people convened around the Astia Message

THE GOLDMAN SACHS 10,000 WOMEN INITIATIVE

Women entrepreneurs around the world are increasing in numbers—statistics from the Global Entrepreneurship Monitor (GEM) 2012 Women's Report show an estimated 126 million women starting or running businesses in 67 countries worldwide.

Launched in March 2008 by the Goldman Sachs Foundation, 10,000 Women was a five-year, $100 million global initiative to foster greater economic growth in developing nations by providing 10,000 underserved women entrepreneurs with business and management education, access to mentors and networks, and links to capital.

10,000 Women was designed to help women grow enterprises in the SME segment and was created to meet four main objectives:

1. Educate 10,000 women
2. Focus on underserved women SME owners
3. Partner with local academic institutions to build capacity in the selected countries
4. Rigorously measure results

Those participating received a comprehensive package of business training, with an average of 180 hours of classroom instruction covering themes such as marketing, accounting, business plan writing, strategic planning, and e-commerce. They also received support including mentoring, business advising, and, in certain countries, access to capital.

Half of the programs were in Africa (Egypt, Liberia, Nigeria, Rwanda, Kenya, Tanzania, and South Africa), three in Asia (China, India, Philippines), two in the Middle East (Turkey and Afghanistan), and three in Central and South America (Mexico, Brazil, Peru).

A report by Babson College[3] analyzing the data collected over the first four years of the initiative demonstrated three main outcomes: revenue and job growth, personal leadership development, and value for the local economy.

Revenue and Job Growth

As Table 21.1 shows, the rate of growth of those participating was impressive.

Table 21.1   Goldman Sachs 10,000 Women Initiative

	Revenue Growth	IFC Country Data	Job Growth	IFC Country Data
Brazil	72.1	7.8	23.8	8.0
China	140.9	10.8	25.3	9.1
Egypt	163.4	n/a	34.6	n/a
India	37.4	n/a	23.2	n/a
Kenya	30.1	13.1	25.9	10.5
Liberia	32.6	n/a	14.8	9.1
Nigeria	365.7	11.5	229.7	10.7
Peru	32.5	8.2	11.0	9.3
Turkey	102.0	13.3	15.9	6.5

Source: "Investing in the Power of Women: Progress Report on the Goldman Sachs *10,000 Women* Initiative." Developed by Babson College (Candida G. Brush, Lakshmi Balachandra, Amy Davis, Patricia G. Greene).

---

[3] "Investing in the Power of Women: Progress Report on the Goldman Sachs *10,000 Women* Initiative." Developed by Babson College (Candida G. Brush, Lakshmi Balachandra, Amy Davis, Patricia G. Greene).

Data was collected in terms of turnover and employee head-count, for a period of 6 to 18 months after graduation; the growth rates were then compared to the national averages for each country (IFC Survey). Though the initial size of the company should be taken into consideration, over one-third of those participating increased their sales by more than 100 percent and recruited an average of four members of staff in the 18 months following the end of the program. These statistics demonstrate the rapid and significant impact of the new skills acquired by the women entrepreneurs during the program.

In addition, it's worth noting that women from developed countries who were mentored also had above-average growth rates for their sector—or when compared to nonmentored women entrepreneurs. Eighty-nine percent of the women interviewed said that their mentor influenced the growth of their businesses, and a similar number (90%) considered that being part of this network of women also had an equally beneficial effect on the growth of their businesses.

Personal Leadership Development

Those participating also reported that their self-confidence, in terms of selling, negotiating and decision making, clearly improved during the course of the program.

Value for the Local Community

Those participating also reported stronger commitments to their local communities and felt inspired to mentor other entrepreneurs—in fact, 90 percent became mentors or advised other women. In this way, around 20,000 more entrepreneurs benefited indirectly from the program.

Conclusions

The outcomes from the 10,000 Women initiative show that the program was both efficient and effective: irrespective of the country, training, and mentoring works.

The outcomes also show the effectiveness and value of a program designed exclusively for women and for the promotion of women's entrepreneurship.

The authors of this report draw four key conclusions:

1. Women can be exceptional entrepreneurs across a diverse array of countries and cultural contexts.
2. 10,000 Women helps entrepreneurs grow their businesses and develop their business acumen.
3. Mentoring, advising, and networks are highly valued in the growth process.
4. Women grow their businesses despite a lack of external financing.

This last point raises another issue: women are more likely to finance their company's growth themselves. Although external financing is needed, women are often reluctant to ask for it—and this caution demonstrates women's aversion to risk. This is particularly regrettable since banks are often ready to finance women's enterprises; indeed, 73 percent of women participating in the initiative obtained a loan when they asked for it.

Entrepreneurship is increasingly recognized as a broad-based driver of economic growth and societal well-being. For women who are primary caregivers, entrepreneurship offers a means to support their families as well. Training and business education for growth-oriented women entrepreneurs is a solution to closing the gender gap in employment, building more prosperous communities, and enabling the growth and development of nations.[4]

---

[4]Babson College Report, 30.

22

Training

___

WOMEN ENTREPRENEUR PROGRAM AT STANFORD

In the summer of 2015, the Stanford Graduate School of Business in California ran the first of many Women Entrepreneur Programs, sponsored by BNP Paribas Wealth Management and designed in conjunction with Women Business Mentoring Initiative. This one-week program attracts women who lead international, fast-growing SMEs in Europe, Asia, and the United States, and provides strategic insight and unique business networking opportunities.

As Sofia Merlo, co-CEO of BNP Paribas Wealth Management said, the program is "a commitment to supporting women entrepreneurship ... and exploring further networking opportunities" and demonstrates the importance major groups and financial institutions place on women and women entrepreneurship, and on motivating and supporting them to success.

These specially designed and narrowly targeted training programs work hand in hand with mentoring, because they enable women to take some distance from their daily work, and see the bigger picture: reflect upon their strategy, develop their leadership skills, navigate the maze of growth opportunities, and find both formal and informal support through professional networking and effective mentoring. As Martine Liautaud comments, programs such as these "provide the foundation stones and building blocks that lead to success" and empower women to reach the highest levels of achievement.

The Stanford Women Entrepreneur Program is delivered by prominent Stanford professors such as Frank Flynn on "Communication and the Art of Persuasion," Bill Barnett on "Innovation as Strategy," Robert Burgelman on "Strategic Leadership: Why It Matters," and Maggie Neale on "Realizing the Synergy of Your Teams." Among a firmament of inspiring talks, we would like to highlight the following: Maggie Neale's message is that "while we are a social species and have been on a variety of different teams all our lives, our organizational teams often under-perform their potential. We will ... identify the behaviors that leaders must model that will facilitate access to the unique information, skills and abilities of team members." Bill Barnett's talk is on how successful businesses happen, and his view is that "the most successful business models are typically discovered, not planned....[which] has implications for how we organize and lead innovative companies." In "Communication and the Art of Persuasion," Frank Flynn talks about how we communicate and says, "The quality of communication largely determines your effectiveness, particularly when you are trying to implement change." And Robert Burgelman addresses the "strategic leadership that senior executives and top management can use to develop the strategic leadership capability of their organization."

The Stanford program in the summer of 2015 was attended by an international group of 30-plus leading women entrepreneurs (see figure 22.1), including U.S. entrepreneurs such as Jackie Robles, general manager of Anita's Mexican Food Corp and winner of the National Small Business Person of the Year Award; Karenjo Goodwin, founder and CEO of Exact Staff, an award-winning staffing company; Nancy Lazkani, president and CEO of Icon Media Direct; Olga Lozano, president of Interstate Home Services, a woman-owned and woman-operated logistics and delivery company; and Jessica Scerri, CEO of Golden State Lumber, which owns four lumber yards in the Greater Bay Area

Figure 22.1   Stanford's Women Entrepreneur Program, Class of 2015.
Source: With the permission of BNP Paribas, sponsor of the program.

of California. Many of the women attending the program testified
that the program was a catalyst for change.

Jackie Robles reported, "I learned new ways of thinking ... and
returned with renewed enthusiasm to apply what I had learned.
It was incredible to meet so many amazing women." Olga Lozano
had similar views: "I was at a crossroads with my own business and
this program showed me how other companies that started small
achieved something big." Martine Liautaud commented that "programs such as these are vital for women scaling up their businesses
and needing the bigger picture to help them take the next steps."

In further interviews with both Jackie and Olga, we asked them
how they became entrepreneurs in the first place. Jackie identified
her parents as her inspiration: "They showed me that perseverance
produces results." For Olga, it was about recognizing her unique
abilities and taking opportunities when they came along: "I was
very good at what I did, and brought a lot of business to my employers. So when an opportunity came along, I decided to branch out on
my own." Naturally both women met obstacles along the way, but

as Olga says, "I believe that the obstacles are only set by our minds; any obstacle seems difficult to overcome, but if you chip away at it, you will gradually overcome it." Jackie's view is similar: "I don't see any obstacles that can't be overcome; but I feel women have to work harder ... and it can sometimes feel as if there is a lack of support, which could create self-doubt if we let it. We just have to have the confidence to stay focused on the goal."

We also asked them what they thought about mentoring and the networking opportunities it brings. Both were enthusiasts, Jackie commenting, "I am a big supporter of mentoring. If I did not receive it, it would have taken me longer to get where I'm at, and it would have been a lot more painful. I've had several mentors, and each one has brought added value and new perspectives." Olga concurs: "I think mentoring is important for women; it's a way of opening women's minds for what they are able to achieve and for growing their possibilities." As Martine Liautaud adds, "With mentoring women can not only reach their goals, but set their goals higher and wider, looking from local to national, and national to global." On networking, Sofia Merlo of BNP Paribas Wealth Management encourages course participants to keep in touch, for instance through social media or further networking events. Jackie's view was that "as an entrepreneur ... networking is essential to success," and both CEOs said they would maintain contact as it was a good way to discuss possible business opportunities and relationships.

The package of "**training + networking + mentoring**"—the message of this book—is essential if we are to unlock the power and potential of women as sources of wealth, as resources for company growth, and as leaders and creators of economic success for nations as a whole. The Stanford program will grow in future years, and we look forward to designing similar programs, offering similar networking opportunities, and implementing similar mentoring programs throughout other regions of the world in order to unlock women's potential in every country.

INDEX